Making Life Work

Putting God's wisdom into action

Bill Hybels

with Lynne Hybels

inter-varsity press

INTER-VARSITY PRESS
38 De Montfort Street, Leicester LE1 7GP, England

Questions for individuals or groups by Andy T. Le Peau.

First British edition 1998
Reprinted 1999

Published in the UK with permission from Inter-Varsity Press, PO BOX 1400, Downers Grove, IL 60515, USA.

British Library Cataloguing in Publication Data

A catalogue record for this book is available from the British Library.

ISBN 0-85110-898-9

Typeset in Great Britain by The Midlands Book Typesetting Company
Printed in Great Britain by Caledonian Intenational Book Manufacturing Ltd, Glasgow

Inter-Varsity Press is the book–publishing division of the Universities an Colleges Christian Fellowship (formerly the Inter-Varsity Fellowship), a student movement linking Christian unions in universities and colleges throughout the United Kingdom and the Republic of Ireland, and a member movement of the International Fellowship of Evangelical Students. For information in about a local and national activities write to UCCF, 38 De Montfort Street, Leicester LE1 7GP.

Making Life Work

Contents

Acknowledgments

My wife, Lynne, redefines the term editor. She lived with this material, pored over it, and prayed over it. To the extent that this content is understandable in written form, the credit goes to her.

My executive assistant, Jean Blount, makes my daily life workable. Her ministry makes mine possible. Thanks, Jean.

This book required some last-minute heroics from some very dear friends: Greg and Corinne Ferguson, Laurie Pederson, and Janice Yarosh. I owe you one!

Finally, the congregation at Willow Creek demonstrated enormous enthusiasm when they heard this material in sermon form. I know no other pastor as deeply indebted to a church family as I am to Willow.

Introduction

Some moments are forever frozen in our consciousness. Such is the moment which gave birth to this book. After a gruelling ten-month run of ministry which had taken me to fifteen foreign countries and countless conferences – in addition to the weekly adventures of leading Willow Creek Community Church – I had finally arrived for my summer break at our little family cottage on the eastern shore of Lake Michigan. There, away from the pressures and incessant demands of ministry, I could recharge my batteries and get some new direction. There I could also pursue my recreational passion of yacht racing, as well as spending quality time with family and friends.

Early one morning, I took my Bible and spiral notebook and headed out for a time of spiritual refreshment, as I have done nearly every morning for the past fifteen years. Eager to read the Scriptures without the cloud of sermon preparation hovering over my head, I flipped through the pages of my Bible until I happened upon the book of Proverbs. *Hmmm. This will do for today*, I thought.

Little did I know . . .

Overlooking the mist-shrouded waters of Lake Michigan, I began reading Proverbs; I didn't stop until I had finished the entire thirty-one chapters. By the time I closed my Bible that morning, I knew I had experienced a 'God Thing.'

I opened my journal and wrote furiously for the next thirty minutes. I knew that day what God wanted me to focus on in my personal study during the next several weeks. I knew that day that the wisdom of Proverbs was going to challenge my mind and heart at a deeper level than ever before. I also had an eerie sense that God might want the truths I discovered in this incredible Old Testament book to touch a wider audience than just me.

By the time I packed up my Bible and journal, the sun was high overhead and the haze had given way to a crystal clear day. The meteorological development of those few hours matched the growing clarity of my thoughts regarding the book of Proverbs; I sensed that its wisdom would figure prominently in my own life and in the life of the church I lead. I was right.

Several months later, at the weekend services at Willow Creek, I began a series of sermons based on Proverbs. I had no idea when I started the series that it would end up receiving a greater response than any other series in the twenty-three-year history of our church. Hundreds of people stood in lines to tell me and other staff members about the amazing impact the practical advice of Proverbs was having on their daily lives. Hundreds more wrote letters detailing the lifestyle changes and spiritual decisions prompted by the weekly addresses. At one point I tried to end the series, but after a near mutiny by our congregation, I extended it for several more weeks.

Why was the book so compelling? Why did it strike such a chord with so many? I believe it comes down to the practical nature of the book of Proverbs that touched people in their everyday decisions and actions. In many different ways the book trumpets out a vital message that gripped them: put God's wisdom into action.

The unity of the message of this colourful book is remarkable, considering that most biblical scholars believe that it is a collection of sayings written by a number of different wise people. The collection was compiled primarily during the period of Israel's history when it was ruled by kings, several hundred years before the birth of Christ. In fact, many of the more than five hundred proverbs are attributed to King Solomon, whom many great minds through the ages have considered the wisest man who ever lived. (For the sake of simplicity, I will sometimes refer to the author of the book of Proverbs in the singular form; please understand, however, that I am actually referring to a group of wise writers.)

Proverbs was not written as a book of promises or rigid rules about life. As it says in the introduction to the book in *The Student Bible*, 'Anybody with a brain can find exceptions to Proverbs' generalities. For instance, Proverbs 28:19 proclaims that "he who works his land will have abundant food, but the one who chases fantasies will have his fill of poverty." Yet farmers who work hard go hungry in a drought, and dreamers win £10 million in the Lottery. *Proverbs simply tells how life works most of the time*. You can worry about the exceptions after you have learned the rule. Try to live by the exceptions, and you court disaster. *The rule is that the godly, moral, hardworking, and wise will reap many rewards*' (p. 561, italics mine).

The Proverbs are written in the poetic forms of the Hebrew culture of that day. Many of them are written in couplets (a pair of successive lines of verse) which make a statement and then repeat it in a slightly different form, as in 8:10, 'Choose my instruction instead of silver, knowledge rather than choice gold.' Or 9:9, 'Instruct a wise man and he will be wiser still; teach a righteous man and he will add to his learning.'

Sometimes the writer drives home his point by setting up contrasts, such as these: 'Do not rebuke a mocker or he will hate you; rebuke a wise man and he will love you' (9:8). Or, 'One man gives freely, yet gains even more; another withholds unduly, but comes to poverty' (11:24).

With their rich and colourful language, certain proverbs paint graphic word pictures. 'As charcoal to embers and as wood to fire, so is a quarrelsome man for kindling strife' (26:21). You can just picture the ease with which a person who loves to pick fights can inflame the emotions of others – it's as easy as throwing dry wood on a blazing fire. Or look at this one: 'Like a roaring lion or a charging bear is a wicked man ruling over a helpless people' (28:15). We can't look at that word picture without knowing exactly how God feels about strong people who take advantage of the weak.

On the other hand, some proverbs are so plain and simple, we almost pass them by – but we shouldn't. Consider this: 'Do not wear yourself out to get rich; have the wisdom to show restraint' (23:4). There's nothing difficult about that verse, but think of how many people have destroyed their lives (not to mention their families) by ignoring its simple wisdom. Or how about this? 'A heart at peace gives life to the body, but envy rots the bones' (14:30). Such a short, inconspicuous word – *envy* – but it has the power to destroy us from the inside out.

The book of Proverbs also has a sense of humour. 'If a man loudly blesses his neighbour early in the morning, it will be taken as a curse' (27:14). Think about being in a university hostel. Your friends party far too late on Friday night. Do you really think they will appreciate your cheerful greeting at 6 a.m. on Saturday? Proverbs is on to you!

Despite its poetic elegance, Proverbs rarely minces words. 'Can a man scoop fire into his lap without his clothes being burned? Can a man walk on hot coals without his feet being scorched? So is he who sleeps with another man's wife; no one who touches her will go unpunished' (6:27–29). Well, that seems pretty clear. How about this one? 'Like a gold ring in a pig's snout is beautiful woman who shows no discretion' (11:22). All right, beauty and indiscretion – not a good match. Or this one? 'Seldom set foot in your neighbour's house – too much of you,

5

and he will hate you' (25:17). Whew! Better not overstay our welcome.

Sometimes the writer addresses unexpected issues: 'A righteous man cares for the needs of his animal, but the kindest acts of the wicked are cruel' (12:10). Who would have thought that how we treat our pets would unmask the truth about our character?

Some proverbs offer hope in times of trial. 'When calamity comes, the wicked are brought down, but even in death the righteous have a refuge' (14:32). 'When the storm has swept by, the wicked are gone, but the righteous stand firm forever' (10:25).

Others are thought-provoking, probing beneath the surface of life. 'Even in laughter the heart may ache, and joy may end in grief' (14:13). 'The purposes of a man's heart are deep waters, but a man of understanding draws them out' (20:5).

Over the weeks that I preached this series, the incisive wisdom of this book authored by a group of ancient Hebrew writers over 2500 years ago seized the heart of our church. Thousands of people fell in love with the down-to-earth poetry of this rich and varied portion of God's Word. The only way I can describe the corporate feeling of our congregation on the final week of the series is to say that there seemed to be an awareness that we were ending a God-anointed era in the teaching ministry of our church. We felt a curious mixture of exhilaration and sadness.

When the idea of putting the Proverbs series into book form emerged, I couldn't help but think back to that summer morning by the lake, when God had so strongly stirred my heart. Of course! He probably had a book in mind all along – oh, me of limited vision and faith.

Now, because of the good people at IVP, you can share in the experience that so gripped me and so touched our church. My only prayer is that at some point throughout your reading, you too will experience a 'God Thing' – a moment of discovery which will freeze time, change your heart, and be long remembered and celebrated as a pivotal point in your ongoing adventure of walking with our great God.

1
Pursue wisdom

Who would have guessed that a series of books ' . . . for Dummies' would sell more than thirty-five million copies? These self-education books have been purchased by people like you and me who wish they knew more than they do about a particular subject. With more than one hundred separate titles in it, the series offers expert advice for just about everyone. Consider a few titles: *Bird-Watching for Dummies, Cocktail Parties for Dummies, Desserts for Dummies, Fishing for Dummies, Investing for Dummies, The Internet for Dummies, Law for Dummies, Parenting for Dummies, Sailing for Dummies,* even *Sex for Dummies.*

Why has this series so effectively tapped into the desire of people to learn? One satisfied customer said: 'I buy them because they take the intimidation out of the learning process. Whatever the subject matter, they spell it out to me in simple terms. They make the complex understandable, so that even an ordinary bloke like me can "get it."'

The same could be said of the book of Proverbs. It takes the ageless, priceless wisdom of God himself and makes it understandable and accessible to ordinary people like you and me. Comprehending its wisdom requires no university degree; the book contains few confusing theological terms. The most down-to-earth book in the Bible, Proverbs puts pertinent truths for everyday life on the bottom shelf where we can all reach them.

Few of the proverbs fit in the category of promises; instead they tell us how life works. One thing they make clear is that, generally speaking, people who are godly, moral, hardworking and wise will reap many rewards. How did the writers know this? They learned it from a lifetime of experience. They were fallible people like you and me who walked with God and pursued his wisdom, messed things up and learned a few hard lessons, observed the successes and failures of others and wrote down their discoveries in order to share them with others.

Above all else, Proverbs is practical. 'A sluggard does not plough in season; so at harvest time he looks but finds nothing' (20:4). You don't plough, you don't eat. Any questions? 'The LORD abhors dishonest scales, but accurate weights are his delight' (11:1). The Lord hates cheating and loves honesty. What part of that one isn't clear?

And how about this passage for proving that the ancient wisdom of Proverbs is in touch with the real world: 'Who has woe? Who has sorrow? Who has strife? Who has complaints? Who has needless bruises? Who has bloodshot eyes? Those who linger over wine, who go to sample bowls of mixed wine. Do not gaze at wine when it is red, when it sparkles in the cup, when it goes down smoothly! In the end it bites like a snake and poisons like a viper. Your eyes will see strange sights and your mind imagine confusing things. You will be like one sleeping on the high seas, lying on top of the rigging. "They hit me," you will say, "but I'm not hurt! They beat me, but I don't feel it! When will I wake up so I can find another drink?"' (23:29–35).

Proverbs is a fascinating and powerful book. As the introduction suggests, where else can we find writing that is poetic yet practical, humorous yet helpful, direct yet deep? Where else can we find the wisdom of God compressed into a few pithy phrases that please our ears and stretch our minds and satisfy our souls?

For what it's worth to you

What is wisdom? Wisdom is what is true and right combined with good judgment. Other words that fit under the umbrella of the biblical concept of wisdom are *discerning, judicious, prudent* and *sensible*. Not very glamorous words, perhaps, but words you can build a life on.

The first nine chapters of Proverbs form an introduction to the remaining twenty-two chapters of the book and present the central message of Proverbs, which is this: *pursue wisdom*. The introduction is written in the warm tones of a fatherly voice giving instructions to his sons and eloquently building a case for the lifelong pursuit of wisdom.

'Listen, my sons, to a father's instruction; pay attention . . . do not forsake my teaching . . . Get wisdom, get understanding . . . Do not forsake wisdom . . . Wisdom is supreme; therefore get wisdom. Though it cost all you have, get understanding . . . accept what I say . . . I guide you in the way of wisdom' (4:1–11).

In verse after verse the father calls his sons to seek wisdom – and then he tells them why. *Because it pays.* 'Blessed', he writes, 'is the man who finds wisdom, the man who gains understanding, for she is more profitable than silver and yields better returns than gold. She is more precious than rubies; nothing you desire can compare with her. Long life is in her right hand; in her left hand are riches and honour. Her ways are pleasant ways, and all her paths are peace. She is a tree of life to those who embrace her; those who lay hold of her will be blessed' (3:13–18).

According to this wise father, those who arrange their lives around the goal of gaining wisdom will receive rewards that far exceed anything they can imagine. You think you want silver? Wisdom is better. You think you want gold? Wisdom is better. You think you want fame, fortune, achievement, power? Wisdom is better. Nothing you desire can compare with her!

Think about the people you know. Do you know any wise parents, fathers and mothers who exhibit sound judgment in how they conduct their lives and raise their children? Do you know any fathers who know when to encourage and when to admonish, when to be tender and when to correct forcefully?

11

Do you know any mothers who know when to give advice and when just to listen, when to teach and when to let life's consequences be their children's teacher? Now try to put a value on those wise insights: How much are they worth? How valuable are they to sons and daughters facing the challenges of the twenty-first century?

I know a lot of clever and hard-working people whose lives are filled with difficulties because they were raised by foolish parents who did not teach them how to make life work. I know many others who are living fulfilling and productive lives. Often they say, 'I grew up in a home with a wise mum and dad.' You can't put a price on the legacy of such parents. Children who grow up with that gift agree heartily with Proverbs 17:6, which says, 'Parents are the pride of their children.'

It works the other way too. How much value would a parent attach to having children who eventually walk in paths of wisdom, who know how to deal with conflict, who handle relationships maturely, who deal with money prudently? You can't put a price on that either. As we read in Proverbs 15:20, 'A wise son brings joy to his father' – and to his mother.

Or consider the workplace. Time and time again I have seen the positive impact of pursuing wisdom. I can think of a number of people I know who have neither dazzling talents, outstanding credentials nor charismatic personalities but who nonetheless have risen to places of strategic importance in business, in government, in academia, in various professions and in the church. These people have gained responsibility and respect for one reason: they have handled themselves wisely in their workplace over a long time. In their work and their relationships on the job, they have applied wisdom from the book of Proverbs – wisdom about taking initiative and developing discipline, wisdom about speaking the truth in love and managing anger and doing good to others. The foolish people around them who neglected these principles eventually fell by the wayside, but these wise people are still at work – and still receiving honour and reward.

This is just as Proverbs says it should be. 'Do you see a man skilled in his work? He will serve before kings; he will not serve before obscure men' (22:29). This means that people who work wisely and skilfully over a long time will be esteemed highly by their peers and superiors, and they will be richly rewarded. Again, this is not a promise or a guarantee, but it is generally the way life works.

Unfortunately, such people are becoming more and more of a rarity. A businessman recently told me that his business was going so well that he couldn't hire salespeople fast enough to take all the orders coming in to his company. 'The only problem', he said, 'is that so many of my new salespeople act strangely.'

'What do you mean by strangely?' I asked.

'I mean they do stupid things and get themselves in trouble. They shoot themselves in the foot. They don't turn up on time. They don't call the people waiting to hear from them. They don't charge fair prices. They don't treat people courteously. They don't admit mistakes when they make them. They don't cooperate with their colleagues. They just act strangely, and eventually I have to sack them. They could be building a successful career. They could be establishing financial security and setting aside a nest egg for the future. Instead, they force me to let them go. I'm not demanding a lot, but how can I tolerate their behaviour?'

What was the bottom line in this man's complaint? 'I can't find enough wise people.' He's frustrated and he's baffled. He knows what wise employees are worth and only wishes he had more.

One of the incomparable benefits of pursuing wisdom is that it offers us a navigational system to keep us out of moral blind alleys and dead-end roads. 'Discretion will protect you, and understanding will guard you. Wisdom will save you from the ways of wicked men, from men whose words are perverse, who leave the straight paths to walk in dark ways' (2:11–13).

Pursuing wisdom is also an effective way of investing in the future. 'If you find it, there is a future hope for you, and your hope will not be cut off' (24:14). What kind of hope does wisdom offer us for the future? Undoubtedly hope for a future in heaven but also, I believe, hope for a life that works . . . here, today, in this world.

That is why I wrote this book. I earnestly believe that the wisdom of Proverbs can make our lives work better. It can offer us invaluable advice about diligence and self-discipline, about choosing friends and boy/girlfriends, about establishing a healthy family life, about honouring God with our finances, about caring for our bodies, about growing spiritually, about caring for the poor, about managing anger and about nearly every other major issue in life.

Bad choices

The writers of Proverbs could have related to my business friend with 'strange' employees. They too were shocked and disgusted by the number of people making unwise choices and ruining their lives. And they didn't hold back in what they had to say about these people. The writers of Proverbs say the opposite of wisdom is foolishness and the opposite of a wise person is a fool.

Today the word *fool* often means someone with low intelligence, but in biblical usage, fools may have a high I.Q. and a reputation for success. What makes them fools is that they ignore God's wisdom, preferring to follow the shifting dictates of the crowd or their own fallible opinions. While fools often consider themselves clever – people who know how to beat the system – their cleverness all too often leads to their ruin. Their penchant for distorting the truth, their lack of discernment and discipline, their unwillingness to exhibit self-control and their apparent delight in throwing caution to the wind put them on a path to disaster.

Folly is what the Bible calls the actions of a fool, and it minces no words in exposing and denouncing both fools and their folly. Repeatedly the Bible warns that the path of a fool is a downward spiral, that folly begets more folly and that the end is destruction. The fool, says the Bible, 'will die for lack of discipline, led astray by his own great folly' (5:23). The fool 'blurts out folly' (12:23). The mouth of the fool 'feeds on folly' (15:14). 'Understanding is a fountain of life to those who have it, but folly brings punishment to fools' (16:22).

In some of the more graphic proverbs we read of the danger of associating with fools: 'Better to meet a bear robbed of her cubs than a fool in his folly' (17:12). We read of the habit-forming nature of fool-ishness: 'As a dog returns to its vomit, so a fool repeats his folly' (26:11). We read of the difficulty of separating a fool from his folly: 'Though you grind a fool in a mortar, grinding him like grain with a pestle, you will not remove his folly from him' (27:22).

Many of the proverbs are parallel constructions that compare the wise and the foolish person. For example, 'The way of a fool seems right to him, but a wise man listens to advice' (12:15). Or, 'A wise man fears the LORD and shuns evil, but a fool is hotheaded and reckless' (14:16). Again, 'A fool gives full vent to his anger, but a wise man keeps himself under control' (29:11).

I wish the Bible wouldn't use words like 'fool' and 'folly' because I hate having to think of myself as a fool, but sometimes I am. Sometimes we all are. Proverbs 22:15 states unequivocally that 'folly is bound up in the heart of a child'. According to the Bible, human beings do not start life with a clean slate. On the contrary, we come into the world with a definite bent toward foolishness.

Think of a chubby baby boy sitting in a sandpit. All a baby knows how to do is act on impulses, so what does the little fellow do when he feels a hunger pang? He grabs a fistful of sand and shoves it into his mouth. He doesn't ask himself if it is wise to have sand for lunch. He just grabs whatever allows him to satiate his hunger pang as quickly as possible, no matter how foolish that option is. If he had been sitting in the yard, he would have had grass or dirt for lunch. Only later does he – and his parents – face the consequences of sand in a baby's belly.

The same instinct for immediate gratification of impulses takes over when young children see something they want. What do they do? They lunge for it. I used to buckle my daughter on the armrest of the car and let her sit beside me while I drove. I would be driving down the main road, and she would become fascinated with the glasses I wear when I drive. Immediately she would tear them off my face. She had no clue about the foolishness of what she was doing. All she knew was that an impulse inside her said, 'Grab!' and like every other little child who has ever been born, her first instinct was to gratify that impulse.

Proverbs tells us what to do about this childish behaviour. 'Folly is bound up in the heart of a child, and the rod of discipline will drive it far from him' (22:15). I do not believe that the 'rod of discipline' implies that we beat foolishness out of a child. The point is that foolishness must be methodically driven out of a child – step by step, month by month, year by year – and replaced by wisdom. That is the only way we can grow out of our infantile folly and become mature people who handle desires and impulses in a godly, constructive way.

A graphic and tragic example of the destructive power of unchecked impulses is the story of the shootings in Jonesboro, Arkansas. Two boys, one aged eleven and one aged thirteen, broke into a relative's house, stole several guns and brought them to a hillside next to their school. Being familiar with how guns work, they properly loaded them, then measured the range to the entrance of the school.

One of them went into the school and sounded the fire alarm. As the children filed out into the car park, the two boys aimed their rifles, wound in their sights and started shooting. Four minutes later, four pupils and a teacher were dead, and ten other people lay wounded in pools of their own blood.

The country was stunned. For weeks the airwaves were filled with the one-word question: Why? Why would two young boys do such a thing? What kind of society are we living in? What has happened to our culture and our values? What systems of thought would produce this kind of behaviour?

According to Proverbs, such behaviour is the inevitable result of living in a world filled with people who are gratifying impulses as foolishly as does a hungry baby in a sandpit. The only difference between the baby in the sandpit and the boys with the guns is that age and circumstances and evil influence had made the gratification of the older boys' impulses deadly.

If anything in the Bible has been proved true, it is that the foolish gratification of impulses will lead to a sick society. We see people gratifying their sexual impulses by engaging in promiscuous sex and committing acts of adultery; we see them acting out twisted desires for power through rape, child sexual abuse and domestic violence. We see people gratifying their desire to possess what isn't theirs through embezzlement, theft, cheating in school or college, and fraud. We see impulse buying, which leads to indebtedness and financial ruin. We see people making impulsive commitments they don't keep and wrecking relationships.

Proverbs says this is nothing but infantile folly and that it is time for those who behave like this to grow up and follow the path of wisdom.

Truth and consequences

One day I met a man in an international airport where we were both nursing our frustrations with air travel. We spent most of the day waiting for planes that never arrived, so we had plenty of time for conversation. He happened to be very angry with God for allowing what he thought was an inordinate amount of pain to enter his life. Since I had plenty of time I said, 'Why don't you tell me your life story?' He was glad to oblige me by unloading his self-pitying saga. What he hadn't counted on was my listening as closely as I did.

When he finished complaining and indicting God for everything that had gone wrong in his life, I said, 'Well, that's quite a story, but could I ask you a couple of questions? You said your former wife turned into a horrible, evil person. I wonder what your relationship with her was like before she became evil. How did you treat her? Were you good to her? Were you faithful to her? Or did you, perhaps, do some stupid things that might have contributed a little to the breakdown of your marriage?' He admitted that he had done a few stupid things.

19

Then I said, 'And about your tens of thousands of pounds of debt and your tax problems with the government – a simple question here. Did you ever let your spending get a little out of hand? Did you ever spend more than you earned? Did you ever buy anything foolishly or impulsively?' He admitted that he had.

Then I said, 'Now you're frustrated because no one will give you a job. Just a question. Were you a model employee? If I called your last three employers, would they be upset over losing an employee as good as you?' Well, he had been sacked from his last job because he had lost his temper a few times and told his boss where to go – eternally.

Finally I admitted that I was a pastor and told him that I didn't believe God had singled him out for special suffering. 'I don't think it's fair to blame him for any of the problems you're blaming him for. The Bible says, "If you sow folly, you will reap heart-break." It seems to me that you've sown plenty of folly and now you're reaping a predictable harvest. My advice to you is to enrol in the school of wisdom today.'

Enrolling in the school of wisdom

I don't know if that man enrolled in the school of wisdom. I would like to think that when he reached his destination at the end of that long day, he looked in the mirror in his hotel room and said, 'You've gone far enough down a foolish path. You've damaged enough relationships, squandered enough time and energy, wasted enough money, said enough stupid words, shed enough unnecessary tears.

You've proved you don't know how to make life work. You've revealed the folly of your ways. It's time to give up on them and seek the wisdom of God.'

Proverbs 1:7 tells him and everyone else what lesson we need to learn first in the school of wisdom. 'The fear of the LORD is the beginning of knowledge.'

Do you want to begin the process of acquiring something that is worth much more than gold? You start by obtaining the knowledge that is most central to the deepest human needs, the knowledge that there is a God who is powerful and personal and head over heels in love with each and every one of us, a God who has extended to us, through Jesus Christ his son, the hand of forgiveness and grace. He says, 'Come on, take that hand, and I'll help you make your life work.' That is where we start.

Some people are tempted to say, 'Yes, you're right. Enough folly. But I don't need God. I'm going in for self-improvement. I'll just start making better choices on my own.' Such people are usually destined to make nearly the same choices in the future as they made in the past. They need to put their hand in God's hand in order to receive a new power to live a new way.

Some time ago, a good friend of mine who has been far from God all his life finally admitted that his own path, his own choices, his own foolish impulses had led him into a terrible mess. In a private setting, he emotionally – and with unprintable expletives – described the collapse of his whole life. He ended with this brief summary statement: 'I have blown it!'

I told him that I couldn't disagree with a word he had said and that the current mess he was in was nothing more than the predictable consequence of twenty-five years of folly. What could he expect after making one foolish choice after the next? 'But,' I said, 'listen to me. There is a way out of your chronic foolishness. You can make a really clever choice in the next five minutes. You can make a choice that is so wise it will redirect what is left of your life here on earth and redirect your entire eternity. If you're ever going to make wise choices, here is where you have to start. Fling open the door of your heart to God; put your hand in the hand Christ has extended to you; accept the forgiveness that is offered to you. The fear of the Lord is the beginning of wisdom.'

Living at peace

The next step from a life of folly to a life of wisdom is to take portions of the Bible, particularly from Proverbs, and apply them to the folly-prone areas and foolish habits of our lives.

Let me explain. When I first became a Christian, an older gentleman said, 'Bill, I can see you're a pretty forceful person. Most likely, whatever you do – whether good or bad – you're going to do with a lot of energy and make a real impact. Why don't you read little portions of the book of Proverbs every day, so that you can learn what is right and what is wrong. Then you can focus your energy towards wisdom and not towards folly.' I was naive, or maybe idealistic, enough to agree to do it. So nearly every day for the first ten years of my Christian life

I read a small section of the book of Proverbs and tried, as best I could, to apply it to my life.

When God led me out of the business world into ministry among young people, I had really to put the wisdom of Proverbs to the test. During my early years at college I had made an unwise decision and had fallen into a sin that I soon regretted deeply and confessed. Some time later, after I had started as a youth leader, I described this secret, embarrassing part of my past to a Christian man whom I thought was a friend. As he coaxed the information out of me, he assured me that 'this is just between the two of us – I'll never tell another soul'. After I disclosed this deeply personal matter to him he prayed for me and thanked me for being vulnerable with him. He told me he considered it a big step forward in our friendship.

Two weeks later I was summoned into the office of my boss, who was calmly preparing to release me from my responsibilities due to some troubling information he had received from – guess who. Not only had my 'friend' fully divulged to my boss everything he had sworn never to tell, but also he had thrown in a few stories of his own creation; they were more than worthy of a spine-tingling soap opera, but they had no resemblance to reality.

He had also told these same exaggerated stories and unfounded rumours to some of the people in the youth group, convincing them that I was a fraud who taught one thing and did another. They would come to me and say, 'Bill, how can you do these things? How can you lie to us?' When I confronted the man, he refused to talk.

23

My boss handled the problem with wisdom and grace, listened to my accurate account of the truth and did not lose confidence in me. The young people also realized eventually that they had been taken in by falsehoods told by someone who had his own twisted reasons for trying to discredit me. So, despite the trauma, in the end both I and my ministry survived.

Still, the hurt from that betrayal lingered in me for a long time. And I didn't just feel hurt; I also felt extremely angry. My deepest impulse was to take matters into my own hands and get revenge. Because I had damaging information about this young man that neither the young people nor my boss had, I knew that I had the power to retaliate and ruin him – and I desperately wanted to. It was a difficult temptation to resist.

But how could I ignore God's wisdom? I had read Proverbs 16:7 a hundred times: 'When a man's ways are pleasing to the LORD, he makes even his enemies live at peace with him.' The first big test I gave God's wisdom was whether God could bring peace into this hostile situation. I knew that my impulse to take the man out to the church car park and release my frustrations with my fists was folly, but God's way was so hard. I clung to this proverb like a sinking person clings to a life jacket in a raging sea. Sometimes I repeated it fifteen to twenty times a day; that was the only way I could keep from doing something stupid.

I kept saying, 'God, help me focus on leading an honourable life, on avoiding slander, on not seeking revenge. Help me to walk in integrity and to trust you to soften his heart and make peace between us one day.'

That did not happen in weeks. It did not happen in months. It did not happen in a year or two years or five years. Eventually the young man drifted away from the youth group, and then I left to start Willow Creek Church. But many years later he called me on the phone and asked me to meet him at a local restaurant for lunch. There he said, 'God has broken me. I have sinned against you so badly. I exaggerated the truth, invented lies and tried to destroy you for reasons I don't even understand, but I know they were dark. God has convicted me of this, and I've gone back to every person I spread those lies to, and I've told them the truth – that you were an honourable person.' Then he reached his hand across the table and said, 'Will you forgive me?'

I drove home after that lunch in awe of the wisdom of God. Proverbs 14:16 says that 'a fool is hotheaded and reckless'. How close I had been to acting like a fool, but God knew that path would have led to an inevitable escalation of anger, resentment and hostility. So he used his word to stop me. His way was hard in that it demanded that I grow up and let go of my immature need to fight folly with folly. It demanded that I give up control of the situation and trust him to work behind the scenes. But it led in the end to reconciliation.

Better broke than bound

For several years after starting Willow Creek Community Church in 1975, I received no salary because the church had no money beyond what was needed to rent a building for our weekend and midweek services. My wife, Lynne, taught private flute lessons, and I worked part-time for my father's greengrocery wholesale business, buying fruit and vegetables on the Water Street Market in Chicago. We were so short of cash that we had to take in lodgers and sell personal possessions. Even then we were dependent on the occasional bag of groceries left anonymously on our front porch. Our kitchen table was a card table borrowed from a friend.

We were staying afloat financially, but only just, and I was getting tired of it, so tired I almost did two things that the Bible clearly says are foolish.

One day a bank sent me an unsolicited credit card. My first thought was, 'My ship has come in! Now I can buy some furniture. Now I can buy some clothes. Enough of this constant doing without.' There was only one problem: Lynne and I would not have the money to pay off the credit card at the end of the month. The idea of buying on credit was sheer folly.

The second thing I almost did was withhold our tithe. All my life I had been taught to give back 10 per cent of whatever income I earned to the local church in order to support God's work. Leviticus 27:30 tells us that 'a tithe of everything from the land, whether grain from the soil or fruit from the trees, belongs to the LORD; it is holy to the LORD'. In Malachi 3:10 God says, 'Bring the whole tithe into the storehouse, that there may be food in my house.' The leaders of the church I grew up in believed that those Old Testament commands should apply to New Testament believers, and so did I. (More on this in chapter ten.) So, throughout high school and college I had tithed, and together Lynne and I had been tithing our meagre income of fifty-five pounds a week. But weren't we justified in giving a bit less than the tithe? Weren't we exceptions?

I was still reading Proverbs nearly every day, and I came upon two proverbs that answered those questions for me. The first verse said, 'The borrower is servant to the lender' (22:7). So there I was, holding a credit card in my hand, while God was saying to me through this little proverb, 'Do you know what's worse than being broke? Being in bondage. Being owned by someone else. Don't add to the pain of financial scarcity by enslaving yourself to debt. Don't do it.'

I cut up the credit card and threw it away.

The second proverb said, 'Honour the LORD with your wealth, with the firstfruits of all your crops [your income]; then your barns will be filled to overflowing, and your vats will brim over with new wine' (3:9–10). That seemed pretty unlikely to me, but what did we have to lose? We were barely making ends meet anyway. I remember asking Lynne to get the chequebook out and write another cheque for £5.50 as our tithe. Whatever happened, we were going to follow the path of wisdom.

I look back on those two decisions and thank God for the book of Proverbs. I realize how seriously the wrong decisions could have affected our family. It was some time before our barns were overflowing – our children often wore second-hand clothes, and for years our only holidays were those provided by gracious friends – but we never lived with the burden of indebtedness, and in time we were so blessed that we could give to others from our abundance and offer more to God's work than the tithe. As a family we have good reason to be committed to the wisdom of Proverbs. Its wisdom has passed the test.

In what areas are you prone to folly? Do you lose your temper easily? Do you break the law in small ways in your business dealings? Do you have relationship problems? Do you not work or study as hard as you should? Do you spend money on frivolous luxuries? Are you undisciplined? Do you lie or distort the truth? Are you proud, glad that you're not like certain other people? Do you struggle with sexual temptations?

Read the book of Proverbs. Find the proverbs that speak to you in the way those I mentioned spoke to me. I guarantee you will find some. Then write them on a piece of paper and put them on your refrigerator, on the dashboard of your car, on your desk at work or school. Read them, repeat them, memorize them, follow them. Cling to them as if your life depends on them. Then see if God doesn't honour your decision to choose wisdom.

We are at the beginning of an adventure in growth. The chapters you are about to read are full of wisdom, not because they are full of my words and thoughts and insights but because they are full of truths straight from the book of Proverbs. I pray fervently that all of you will sign up for this adventure and enrol in the school of wisdom and that this exploration of Proverbs will be a time in your life when you turned from folly to wisdom and found the treasure that is better than gold.

2
Take initiative

A wealthy man once entrusted his entire financial
estate to the care of a financial agent. The agent did
quite well for a while, but word then came back to
the rich man that the agent was getting a little careless with his resources. The rich man responded
quickly and unequivocally. 'I don't like what I hear,'
he told his employee. 'Here's your P45.'

The agent panicked; he knew that after years in a
desk job he was ill-prepared for manual work, and
he was too proud to beg in the streets. What could
he do? How could he make a living?

Eventually his desperate and scheming mind
devised a creative plan. He went to two of the people
who owed his boss money and offered to reduce the
debts. The agent said to the first, 'Take what you
owe, sit down quickly, and write a bill for half the
amount.' He told the second debtor, 'Take your bill
and cut it by twenty percent.'

He offered these discounts in the hope that after he lost his job the creditors would think positively about him and offer him help until he could get back on his feet professionally; perhaps they would let him live in their guest house for a while or provide a list of potential business contacts. The agent offered the discounts, the debtors paid their reduced debts, and the agent lost his job.

As Jesus told this parable (found in Luke 16), I can imagine his audience listening politely to this story, as we would, and patiently waiting for the punchline. Then it comes, and I can see the crowd raising an uproar, as readers of this parable have been doing for two thousand years.

Why? Because the master in the story didn't condemn his servant. Instead he commended the actions of the financial agent! How could he do so?

Although it is true that the agent didn't actually pocket his master's money, he cheated his employer out of a portion of it for his own benefit. That's hardly commendable behaviour. Yet when the master heard about what his dishonest former agent had done, he said in essence, 'I've got to hand it to you. You were in a tight corner. You knew that losing your job at this stage in your life was a serious problem. So you looked at some options. You took action. You solved your problem. You are to be commended.'

Obviously this parable is not about ethics. In fact, in this passage Jesus describes the agent as dishonest and places him squarely within the category of 'people of this world', a group that he contrasts with 'people of the light' who walk in honesty, integrity and godliness. Still, Jesus commends the man for something he obviously considers extremely important: he commends him for taking the initiative to solve his problem.

It seems like common sense, doesn't it? If we have a problem, we need to think of a solution and then implement it. What else is there to do?

But the truth is, all too few people do it. It's much easier to sit and complain about the unfairness of life or the overwhelming frustrations of the modern world. Why take initiative in solving our problems when we have the fashionable option of blaming our parents, our spouse, our friends, our employer, our teachers, our government or our God for our problems?

Another alternative to taking initiative is to settle into a mushy belief in some better future that is eventually going to 'just happen' to us. Underlying many lifetimes of inactivity is an unspoken but deeply held belief that goes something like this: Somehow, one day my life will improve. Somehow, one day I'll drift into more satisfying circumstances. Somehow, one day what I want will come to pass. Built on the fantasy that rewards will come without hard work, this notion is closer to a wistful hope than a considered philosophy, more akin to a child's belief in magic than an adult's grasp of reality. But it's a mindset that is pervasive.

Somehow, one day ... I'll feel like doing something with my life ... I'll start waking up earlier ... I'll stop wasting so much time at parties ... I'll start getting my essays done on time ... my boss will notice me ... I'll stumble into the job of my dreams

. . . the perfect spouse will float into my life . . . the credit card companies will lose my records . . . I'll win the Lottery . . . my marriage will transform itself . . . my children will stop getting into trouble . . . my metabolism will increase and the fat will melt away . . . I'll stop craving another drink . . . I'll start wanting to help the poor . . . I'll feel like being a serious Christian.

Somehow, one day . . . it'll just happen.

Are you sure? Have you seen life work this way? I've seen the opposite. The natural movement in life tends to be down, not up. Those who choose to sit back and go with the flow normally end up going downhill. That's not to say there's anything wrong with a relaxing float down a mountain stream now and then, but if you ever want to see the view from the peaks, you're going to have to climb back up that mountain. Without a doubt that uphill walk is going to require action and initiative, and nobody who has embraced the 'somehow, one day' philosophy will ever reach the peaks.

I'll do it . . . tomorrow

The book of Proverbs calls people who live according to this philosophy *sluggards*. An endearing little term, isn't it? A slug is a slimy snail-like creature that has no shell. Imagine a slug rolling along on its slow, purposeless journey. Watch it bump into a pebble and come to a dead stop. See it pushed backward by the force of a wave. Makes me want to tell it to give up – but it probably already has.

Sluggards are, in a word, lazy. 'How long will you

lie there, you sluggard?' asks the wise man in Proverbs. 'When will you get up from your sleep? A little sleep, a little slumber, a little folding of the hands to rest – and poverty will come on you like a bandit and scarcity like an armed man' (6:9–11). In this case the sluggard's laziness leads to poverty, but financial difficulties are usually just one manifestation of the sluggard's ruin.

The book of Proverbs says that many of us are in danger of becoming sluggards, and it describes a progression that could and probably would put us on the sluggard's futile and fruitless path. The first step down that path is procrastination. Every time a person responds to a pressing responsibility with a careless 'I'll do it later,' he or she is acting in a sluggardily way.

When I was a child and my mother asked me to set the table or take out the rubbish, I was likely to say something like, 'At the next commercial break, Mum,' or 'As soon as I've finished putting this model together.' If my father heard me, he'd say, 'Do it now, Billy. Don't wait.' That aggravated me at the time; I thought he was unnecessarily inflexible and unreasonable. Now I realize he was a wise man who was committed to steering his son off the path of the sluggard. How grateful I am that as an adult I never had to go through the pain of breaking the pattern of procrastination. My father did me a huge service by demanding prompt and responsible action.

Making excuses

The second step down the increasingly slimy path of the sluggard is to make excuses. Let's say that on the way to work in the morning an able-bodied worker remembers a challenging responsibility she didn't have time to complete the previous day. That worker could use her journey time to pray and ask God for strength. She could think about creative ways of fulfilling that responsibility more efficiently. She could decide to face that daunting task with as much energy and aggressiveness as she can muster. But if she's on the sluggard's path, she'll choose a different option. She'll find an excuse for not facing that challenge or not accepting the responsibility – perhaps, even, for not going to work that day.

The sluggard quoted in Proverbs 22:13 comes up with a great reason for not going to work. 'There is a lion outside!' he says. To make sure no one questions his admirable reason for remaining within the safe and undemanding confines of home, he adds, 'I will be murdered in the streets!' Well, maybe. Or maybe his imagination is just a bit more vivid than that of the average excuse-maker. Maybe he finds it more stimulating to conjure up a fascinating list of everything that could go wrong than patiently to work his way through the mundane list of tasks to be completed or responsibilities to be accepted.

And what if there *is* a lion in the streets? The man should join the lion hunt! Only a sluggard would sit around for the rest of his life because there are dangerous obstacles in his way. There will always be lions in the street. There will always be frightening responsibilities. There will always be overwhelming challenges. There will always be heartbreaking disappointments. But only the sluggard will make excuse after excuse in the face of life's demands.

Think about your own life. Do you make excuses for lack of performance, lack of diligence, lack of discipline, lack of any good thing? If so, the book of Proverbs offers you a clear warning. Procrastination breeds procrastination. Excuses breed excuses. Laziness, sluggishness, indolence, slothfulness, whichever slow-moving word you choose – they all breed more and more and more of the same slimy stuff. It's a thick soup you're sinking into, and you'll end up stuck in a life of ruin.

Proverbs 19:24 describes such a life like this: 'The sluggard buries his hand in the dish; he will not even bring it back to his mouth!' In this humorous exaggeration, he drops his hand in his bowl of food and has neither the energy nor the motivation to lift it out.

Proverbs 26:14 says, 'As a door turns on its hinges, so a sluggard turns on his bed.' Back and forth he shifts, restlessly rolling from one side of his bed to the other. But he goes nowhere; he's as stuck as a door on a hinge.

The Nine-out-of-ten Club

What about you? Is the book of Proverbs beginning to convict you? Have you taken more steps down the sluggard's path than you care to admit? Have you developed a pattern of procrastination or become too quick to make excuses? Have you traded initiative and diligence and perseverance for sluggishness and indolence and slothfulness?

Or are you like most of the people in my circle of acquaintances and friends, who say, 'Are you joking? Slothfulness is the least of my problems. I

35

couldn't find the sluggard's path if I wanted to. In fact, I'd probably be better off if I did procrastinate now and then. An excuse or two may be just what I need. I already have more than enough activities to be involved in, people to help, work to do. Too busy is what I am – not too lazy.' Indeed, these high-powered types seem to have little in common with the lowly sluggard.

'You'll never see me sitting around with folded hands', they say, 'or complaining about lions in the streets. And for goodness' sake, don't worry about my eating habits; I've never once left my fingers lying in my food. Nor have I ever rolled from side to side like a door on a hinge. Me a sluggard? Not a chance!'

If you had the motivation and energy to pick up this book and read this far, you've probably not sunk into the ugly quagmire of comprehensive sluggardliness, universal inactivity or across-the-board slothfulness. If the truth be told, few people I know have sunk that low.

But that doesn't mean we have nothing to learn from the sluggard. In fact, I believe that many of us who on the surface look like models of industry and diligence are suffering from a hidden disease called selective sluggardliness, a disease characterized by carefully constructed compartments where slothfulness reigns. These little pockets of laziness or inactivity, though seemingly insignificant and nearly always unseen by others, will ultimately bring pain and heartache, even ruin, into our lives.

What kind of people suffer from selective sluggardliness?

- The student who succeeds athletically and socially but fails to take seriously the education of his or her mind.

- The father who sets sales records at work and has a four handicap on the golf course but fails miserably to respond to the emotional needs of his wife and children.

- The mother who pours herself out on the job and on the home front but who continually neglects her relationship with God.

- The men and women who fill their time with people but never tend the soil of their own interior lives. They never look deeply at the emotional and psychological realities that drive their behaviour, affect their goals and shape their relationships.

- It's those who spend more money than they have and say tomorrow they'll go on a budget – but tomorrow never comes.

- It's church members who nod their heads when the pastor challenges them to a deeper commitment to God, but when Monday morning rolls around they're back to being casual Christians.

One reason selective sluggardliness is so deadly is that if other areas of our lives look good enough we can convince ourselves that we deserve to be let off the hook. 'For crying out loud, I'm taking initiative and working diligently in nine-out-of-ten areas of my life. Isn't that good enough? What are you asking for, perfection?'

I know a little girl in Promiseland, the Sunday

school at my church, who has endured more than her share of life's hardships. Some of her few joys are the relationships she has with her Promiseland teacher and the other children in her class. Her father, whom I have known for many years, recently decided that he'd rather sleep for an extra hour on Sunday mornings than take his little girl to church.

If this man wants to be lazy, that is his choice; but I hated what his laziness was doing to his little girl. So I decided to talk to him. 'Listen,' I said, 'I may have no right to tell you how to live your life, but what's happening in your little girl's life is breaking my heart. She needs to be reminded every week that God loves her, she needs the care of a loving Christian teacher, and she needs the fun and fellowship offered by Christian friends. She's not going to get any of that unless you take the initiative and get her to Promiseland. You're an adult and you can decide what to do with your life, but what you do with this precious little girl God has entrusted to your care … well, someone has to speak for her.'

He said, 'Come on, Bill. Give me a break. I work hard. I travel during the week. I help my friends. I vote. I follow the rules. I'm a decent bloke. But I get tired. I need a day off.'

He was trying the nine-out-of-ten excuse, and I wasn't buying it. 'Nine out of ten may be fine for you', I told him, 'if that's how you want to live. But the tenth part is about your daughter. Get lazy in another area. Don't get lazy in an area that affects the life and eternity of a precious little girl.' Maybe he had only one area of laziness, but he was playing with high stakes.

My father died of a heart attack at the age of fifty-three. A larger-than-life character, he was one of the most energetic and motivated men I have ever known; few people could even begin to keep up with him. He started businesses, helped with church work, flew aeroplanes, rode motorcycles and sailed a forty-five-foot yawl across the Atlantic Ocean. *Take Initiative* could have been his life's motto.

He was disciplined and diligent in every area of his life, except one: caring for his body. He was lazy and careless about that all his life. He paid no attention to diet or exercise. Nine out of ten isn't bad – unless the tenth one kills you.

A certain Old Testament leader was highly respected. Most people considered his life a model of how to live with integrity. But in his later years his life and ministry fell apart because of one area of laziness.

The leader's name was Eli, and his area of selective sluggardliness was that he wouldn't discipline his sons. He had two boys who were little rascals, and though he intended to train them in the ways of godliness and integrity, it proved to be a more daunting challenge than he had anticipated. So he gave up.

In time his little rascals became big rascals. The trouble they eventually caused led to Eli's undoing. Again, nine out of ten. But the tenth one brought him down.

Visit the Ant College

Most of us, if we dare to look beneath the veneer of our lives, can find at least one pocket of sluggardliness, one little area of carelessness or laziness. What should we do when we see it?

A classic passage in Proverbs answers that question by having the lazy slug take a look at its industrious counterpart. 'Go to the ant, you sluggard; consider its ways and be wise! It has no commander, no overseer or ruler, yet it stores its provisions in summer and gathers its food at harvest' (6:6–8).

The wise and witty writer of the Proverbs comes through again. 'Do you want to learn about initiative? Do you want to become more diligent? Then enrol in the Ant College. That's right. That lowly creature you squash on the pavement knows a few things about life that you need to learn.'

First, the ant knows that if you have to depend on external motivation to get the job done, you're in trouble. If you have to depend on a boss, an officer, a teacher or a ruler to keep you moving, what are you going to do when there's no one looking? The secret, I think, to the ant's self-motivation is that it keeps its goal in mind all the time. Food, food, food. It pictures the delicious morsels in its mind. It imagines the gnawing pain of an empty stomach. It reminds itself that if it doesn't harvest and store provisions, it won't eat. Why should the ant need an external force pleading and prodding when it is so single-minded about its goal?

The second lesson we need to learn in the Ant College is that the ant thinks ahead. It comes up with a plan and decides what needs to be done and when. It knows that if it wants provisions through the winter it'll have to work hard during the summer. Once an ant gets its plan and timetable worked out, it motivates itself into action. The ant doesn't procrastinate. It doesn't make excuses. It says in its little voice, 'Let's get going. Let's get to work. Let's do it now.'

In the remainder of this chapter I want to highlight five areas of life in which we need to manifest the initiative and diligence of the lowly but wise ant. I want to challenge you to read the next few pages in a spirit of submission to God and to listen carefully to what he is saying he wants you to do. The Holy Spirit can be trusted to give you insights regarding these areas of life, even if you are a new Christian or an enquirer who has not yet become a Christian.

It may be that as you read about one of these areas the Holy Spirit will say to you, 'You're putting plenty of initiative into this area. Everything's fine. Keep up the good work.' If that's what you hear from the Spirit, then relax.

It may be, however, that when you read about a different area the Holy Spirit will say to you, 'Listen carefully. You know this area is a problem for you. You know it's time to take some initiative and work with diligence. It's time to get off the sofa and on to the playing field. It's time to move forward.' If that's what you sense, pay attention. Take seriously that inner voice of guidance and challenge. Surrender to it.

Making peace

The first area is highlighted by some of the best-known and best-loved words in the Bible. In the apostle Paul's first letter to the Corinthians he writes, 'And now these three remain: faith, hope and love. But the greatest of these is love' (1 Corinthians 13:13). Contrary to much that we hear in the popular media of our materialistic culture, the greatest legacy we humans can leave is the legacy of love. Whether we're speaking of our place within society at large or in the context of our most important relationships, the most valuable gifts we can offer are those thoughts and actions that flow from a loving heart.

It is within the context of the family that loving actions are most appreciated and necessary – and most difficult to maintain. We all have good intentions, but in the rough-and-tumble of life we tend to bump and bruise each other. Even little wounds to our egos or our souls hurt, and often our natural reaction is to withdraw.

As emotional distance increases so does resentment. Soon a relationship of love has become a breeding ground of ill feelings. We know we should put an end to the discord. We should talk to the other person and try to resolve the problem. But we know how much time and energy it will take and how frustrating it may be. We know a real solution will probably require a long period of effort rather than a single conversation. One more big effort is the last thing we need right now. We're already too busy. Life is already too complicated.

So we yield to the temptation of selective sluggardliness. We get lazy when it comes to relationships. We give up. We don't make the phone call. We don't write the letter. We don't walk across the corridor in the college hostel, across the factory floor at work or across the aisle at church. We don't hold out the hand or say the gentle word or take the time to listen. Rather than taking initiative in pursuing reconciliation or a deeper relationship, we close our eyes and sleep the destructive sleep of the sluggard.

Romans 12:18 says, 'If it is possible, as far as it depends on you, live at peace with everyone.' 'If it is possible' implies a tenacity that doesn't give up because the process of reconciliation or growth is difficult and demanding or even strewn with seemingly insurmountable obstacles; it implies a willingness to cling to the last shred of hope and to move forward in acknowledgment of that hope.

'As far as it depends on you' implies that we cannot control another person's response to our peace initiative. Sometimes our most sincere efforts will be ineffective because of someone else's refusal to co-operate. Though that may be extremely frustrating, it does not relieve us of responsibility. The questions remain for us: Have I taken the initiative? Have I done my best? Have I gone as far down the road of reconciliation as I can?

A number of years ago the marriage of a friend of mine entered a difficult phase. Eventually he tired of working on the relationship, and he divorced his wife. Last summer I took a long walk with him. I wish I could play a tape recording of our conversation. 'I gave up the most important relationship in my life because of laziness,' he said. 'That's all it was. If I could, I'd put the clock back and start again. And this time I wouldn't stop working at the relationship.'

Another man wrote to me, 'Being on my own, divided from my children, has torn a hole in my heart that just doesn't heal. Dealing with the pain of loss is harder than the relationship ever was. I wish I hadn't given up so easily.'

If these words prompt you to take more initiative and show greater diligence in relationships, please do so. The stakes are high; the pain of loss is great. Yes, your efforts at reconciliation may be rebuffed, but more often than not they will be warmly welcomed and met with a sincere 'I want to try too. Thanks for taking the initiative.'

Plain hard work

The wise man of Proverbs had a positive perspective on work, the second area I'd like you to consider. He saw work as the secret of financial success, the pathway to freedom and the expression of creativity. 'All hard work brings a profit,' he said, 'but mere talk leads only to poverty' (14:23). 'Diligent hands will rule, but laziness ends in slave labour' (12:24). The apostle Paul takes this positive view of work a step further when he reminds us that our ultimate reason for working diligently is to honour our true boss. He says, 'Whatever you do, work at it with all your heart, as working for the Lord, not for men' (Colossians 3:23).

Here's the question: Are you 'working with all your heart' at your place of employment, at home, at college? I am not asking if you're expending the necessary energy to do the tasks assigned to you. I am asking if you are doing every project that comes your way to the best of your God-given potential, as if you were doing it for God himself, not just for your earthly boss. I am asking if you are displaying the best possible character as you work. At your company, are you setting the standard for ethics, honesty, love, conscientiousness, excellence and promptness? Are you demonstrating genuine concern for those you work with, even pointing them to Christ if you get the opportunity?

I know what it's like. When you've been in the same job for some time, it's easy to develop bad habits, to take short cuts, to settle for minimum productivity, to engage in destructive chatter, to criticize the boss, to stir up dissension, to undermine other people's efforts and to engage in subtle forms of self-promotion. Seldom do we start out that way, and often we're not aware of the steps we've taken; the changes in our thinking, our speaking and our acting have been so slight we have barely noticed them. But an honest look reveals that we're not the workers we once were. No longer are we models of industry and integrity in the workplace.

Or perhaps some of us never were. Perhaps we fall within that category of irresponsible and misguided people who think they can get out of doing any diligent work. People who think that they can somehow cheat the system and get a comfortable life for themselves without ever having to work for it. People who think they deserve good fortune or believe the fantasy that life is supposed to be easy; if they have to work hard, then something must be wrong. Such thinking is called immaturity. The truth is that life is difficult and making a living is difficult. Our work, we hope, is generally fulfilling and meaningful, but there are bound to be aspects of it that are just plain hard. There will be days when we do our work because we love it, and other days when we do our work simply because we don't like to give up. That's real life, for all of us.

Is the Holy Spirit quietly and gently telling you there's room for change in this area? Do you need to take some initiative – immediately – to change the way you work so you can do so with all your heart, as for the Lord? The wisdom of the Bible says that diligent workers will be rewarded by their peers, by their employers and by God. This is no glib promise of health and wealth and happiness; it's a simple but profound insight about the way life works. Diligent work is the pathway to a meaningful, responsible and useful life.

Fuel for the race

I know I'm about to interfere seriously in people's lives with this third topic, but too often this important issue of our physical well-being is ignored. A sobering passage for those of us who are Christians is found in 1 Corinthians 6:19–20: 'Do you not know that your body is a temple of the Holy Spirit, who is in you, whom you have received from God? You are not your own; you were bought at a price. Therefore honour God with your body.' Could the point be stated more clearly? Our bodies are temples of the Holy Spirit. We need to honour God with our bodies.

How is it that we manage to separate the issue of how we treat our bodies from our devotion to Christ? Not just our spirits but also our bodies have been bought with a price. Not just our spirits but also our bodies have been claimed and redeemed and loved. Christianity does not teach a view of life that disdains the body while it elevates the spirit. In some mystical and incomprehensible way the Holy Spirit indwells our bodies and thereby calls us to the great privileges and major responsibility of using our bodies to honour his presence.

What does it mean to honour God with our bodies? It means we pay attention to where we take our bodies, whom we let touch our bodies, how we take care of our bodies. It means we keep our bodies away from sin, we protect them from abusive people and circumstances, and we actively pursue physical health. Maintaining sexual purity is one specific means of honouring God with our bodies, as is avoiding nicotine, excessive alcohol and caffeine, or any other drugs or substances that could harm them.

Honouring God is about exercising, not compulsively nor in an unhealthy attempt to measure up to our culture's standard of attractiveness but in order to increase our energy and longevity. It is also about eating the proper amounts of natural, nutritious foods. When I did motorcycle racing, I learned that if I wanted to compete well in a race I had to get the finest racing fuel I could find, strain it meticulously and then fill the tank with it. Anything less than that would inhibit the performance of the bike. The same is true for us. Our bodies are God's greatest creation, but we can't expect them to perform at their best unless we use the highest-quality fuel.

What is the Spirit saying to you about your body? What are you saying back? Few challenges in life are met with as many excuses as our responsibility for caring for our bodies. One Sunday, after addressing this issue in my sermon, I felt so burdened about one of my church leaders that I had to hold back the tears when I watched him walk down the side aisle. 'Don't do what my father did,' I told him later. 'Don't kill yourself by neglecting your body. For God's sake and for the sake of your family and friends, please don't do that.'

Our bodies are so alive with conflicting desires, so attuned to pleasures and pains, so tempted by immediate gratification. Responding in a God-honouring way to these natural drives and desires requires more discipline and determination than almost anything else. It also requires a conscious submission to God's purpose for our lives, which is to be a pure dwelling place for his own Spirit. It's not easy to keep such an intangible notion in mind, nor is it easy to perform the tangible acts that keep our bodies pure and healthy. But whatever progress we make towards honouring God with our bodies will bring us direct benefit. Our self-esteem will increase, along with our physical and mental energy, and our relationship with God will be improved. We can't lose.

Money matters

We've considered relationships, work, health. A fourth area of potential laziness is the way we handle money, whether we have a little or a lot. Some people with limited resources think they have too little to worry about. What difference will it make if they let a few pounds slip through their fingers here and there? Even the most responsible stewardship wouldn't transform their tiny pile of cash into anything worth shouting about, so why bother?

Let me say it as kindly as I can: That's twisted

thinking. The only way to increase limited resources is through meticulous stewardship and aggressive initiative.

At the opposite end of the continuum are those people with too much money who think they don't have to bother about careful money management because there's always plenty of money to meet their commitments; they never have to worry about a missed mortgage payment or a material need that isn't being met, so why worry about it?

What they're forgetting is that how we handle money matters. It matters to God, who sees it as one indication of our personal maturity and our obedience to Christ. It matters to our children, who learn how to handle money from watching how we handle it. It matters to the poor, whose state of health and well-being may hinge on our generosity. It matters to the church, whose God-honouring purposes will be either thwarted or facilitated by the giving of God's people. We cannot afford, you see, to be lazy when it comes to money matters. There is too much at stake.

Jesus said to those with little means, 'Whoever can be trusted with little can also be trusted with much' (Luke 16:10). Can we justify carelessness because the amounts are small? On the contrary. Be faithful with little, says Jesus, and one day you will have opportunity to prove your faithfulness with greater things. I don't know whether the 'much' of Jesus' statement indicates an increase in financial resources, an increase of some other kind of responsibility in the kingdom or an increase in growth and faith. I suspect it means all three, but what does it matter? Jesus calls us to be faithful in little and promises a reward that he deems worthy. What greater incentive do we need?

Paul was speaking of those on the other end of the continuum when he said, 'Command those who are rich in this present world not to be arrogant nor to put their hope in wealth, which is so uncertain, but to put their hope in God, who richly provides us with everything for our enjoyment. Command them to do good, to be rich in good deeds, and to be generous and willing to share' (1 Timothy 6:17–18). Wealth is a gift from God, not to be hoarded and made our hope, not to be trusted as security, but to be freely enjoyed and generously shared and used as a tool for any number of good deeds.

Is God talking to you about money matters just now? Have you been careless with your little? Have you taken it lightly and frittered it away? Have you been careless with your much? Have you used it selfishly and withheld a potential blessing to others? Remember that your money matters to God, to your children, to the poor and to the ministry of the church. Respond to the Spirit's prompting. God will bless you.

Rich towards God

The last area I want to consider in connection with taking initiative is our relationship with God. I want to set the scene for this topic by looking at a passage in the Gospel of Luke in which a man asked Jesus to command his brother to divide the family inheritance with him. Jesus took advantage of the opportunity to do a little teaching about life. 'Watch out!' he said to his crowd of listeners. 'Be on your guard against all kinds of greed; a man's life does not consist in the abundance of his possessions' (Luke 12:15).

Jesus continued his teaching about what is and is not important in life by telling a story about an extremely successful and wealthy farmer/business-man. The man's fields produced abundant crops, and the man knew how to make the most lucrative deals with the wholesalers. He loved his work, he was fired up by it, and everything he did seemed to turn to gold. It may well be that along the way he received quiet promptings to develop his spiritual life, but apparently he considered doing bigger and bigger deals a more valuable use of his time and energy than seeking God.

The man's fields continued to produce spectacu-larly. His business grew beyond his wildest dreams. Eventually he had to tear down his barns and build bigger ones to hold all his grain and goods. Bursting with satisfaction, he said to himself, 'You have plenty of good things laid up for many years. Take life easy; eat, drink and be merry' (Luke 12:19).

What a pity that the man didn't get to read the next verse before he experienced it: 'But God said to him, "You fool! This very night your life will be demanded from you."' What good did his barn full of grain and goods do him then? What good did all his deals do? He had invested his time and energy in storing up mountains of riches, but he had invested nothing in what mattered most, and he stood before God empty-handed. Jesus concluded the story of that man's life with a cryptic summary: 'This is how it will be with anyone who stores up things for himself but is not rich towards God' (Luke 12:20–21).

I like that phrase 'rich towards God'. What does it mean to be rich towards God? I think it means to give God what he desires most, which is a relationship with us. Some of us give ourselves lavishly and freely – richly! – to all sorts of people, activities, achievements and responsibilities. We devote our time, energy, creativity and attention to our education, work, friends, families and pleasures. But we forget about God. We never consider what it means to be rich towards him.

In another passage, Jesus asks his followers, 'What good is it for a man to gain the whole world, yet forfeit his soul? Or what can a man give in exchange for his soul?' (Mark 8:36–37). The rich man discovered he couldn't trade his riches for his soul. What about you? What about your soul? Have you been pouring all your time and energy into building bigger barns while neglecting your relationship with God? Don't make the mistake the rich man made. Take the initiative in becoming rich towards God. Whether you're at the beginning of your spiritual journey or have stopped at a roadblock along the way, decide now on the next step you need to take. Do you need to be more disciplined in personal reflection and prayer, in studying the Bible and other Christian literature, in fellowship with Christians and in regular church attendance? Decide on your next step, and then take it. Commit yourself to spiritual initiative. In return you'll receive something that will last for all eternity.

Divine initiative

The archetype of one who takes initiative is God himself. He created the heavens and the earth, spinning into motion the tiny sphere that is our planet. He filled its waters and skies with fish and birds and scattered all manner of living creatures across its mountains, valleys and plains. Then he lovingly spoke humankind into being, calling man and woman to name the animals, to tend to the garden which was spread out at their feet and to live in loving community with one another.

But then he watched as man and woman disobeyed him, dishonoured themselves and destroyed each other with hatred and lies and murder. He watched his creation spiral deeper and deeper into sin; he felt the searing pain as those made in his very image pulled away from him, breaking the bonds of love that had bound creature to creator. How easy it would have been for him to yield to despair and to close his eyes to the ugly ruin his creation had become.

But what did he do? He responded with love and with a plan. He provided a solution to the problem. He took the initiative in bridging the gap between himself and his wayward creation. 'For God so loved the world' – and longed to have it reconciled to himself – 'that he gave his one and only Son, that whoever believes in him shall not perish but have eternal life' (John 3:16).

God could have sat idly by and watched the world go to hell. But love demanded that he take the initiative to redeem it instead. So he sent his only son,

Jesus Christ, as a sacrifice for your sin and mine, thereby making forgiveness available as a free gift. We need only to humble ourselves enough to receive it.

Is that the next step that spiritual initiative demands of you? Or as you've read this chapter has God been prompting you in one of the other areas I've mentioned? Whatever it is, don't hesitate, don't wait, don't delay. Decide now. Take action.

3
Do good

I may have established a new record the day I spent eighteen hours travelling on a commercial aircraft from Chicago to Los Angeles. Though I clearly remember everything that went wrong that day, I'll spare you the details. Suffice it to say that after two delayed flights and six hours sitting on runways in packed planes, I was in no mood to discover that the flight that marked the final leg of that tedious journey had just been cancelled. Nor was I too enthusiastic about standing in a queue with two hundred other irate people who were as impatient as I was to sort out the whole mess. Sorting it out included a frantic run from one end of an airport to the other in a desperate attempt to grab a seat on one more overbooked flight – the last possible connection to California that night.

Anyway, I finally got on the aeroplane and collapsed into my seat. My hand luggage was on my lap because there was no room in the overhead lockers or under the seats. The only thing I wanted to do was sin. I was thinking bad words, and I wanted to say them, but I choked them back because supposedly I am a godly man. I was repeating Proverbs 17:28, which says, 'Even a fool is thought wise if he keeps silent.' I knew there was nothing godly about me at that moment, but at least if I kept my mouth shut I could pretend to be wise.

We were ready to back away from the boarding gate when a woman rushed through the door and began stumbling down the aisle. She was carrying an assortment of bags that were spilling all over the place, but that was the least of her problems. What made her situation nearly impossible was that she had one eye literally sewn shut, and she seemed to be unable to read her seat number with her other eye. The flight attendants were nowhere to be seen, undoubtedly huddled in the back playing cards – I was thinking the worst about everybody by that time.

I was fuming and feeling sorry for myself when God brought to my mind a proverb that I had read a few weeks earlier. The most disturbing thing about some of these pithy verses in Proverbs is that once you get them in your mind, you can't get them out; they keep coming back to haunt you. There I was, wanting to be completely self-absorbed and hateful, and God whispered in my ear, 'Your own soul is nourished when you are kind; it is destroyed when you are cruel' (Proverbs 11:17 Living Bible).

The voice in my head went on: 'All right, Bill, I know this has not been one of your good days.

You've missed flights, and waited on the tarmac, and stood in queues, and you've hated it. You're feeling pretty knocked about and frustrated. But now you've got a chance to make it a better day by getting out of your seat and showing kindness to a desperate woman. I won't make you do it, but I think you'll be pleasantly surprised if you do.'

Part of me was saying, 'I don't think so. I'm not in the mood.' And it was saying it loudly. But another part of me was saying, 'Maybe my mood has nothing to do with it. Maybe I should just do it.' So I got up, walked down the aisle and asked the woman if I could help her read her seat number. She seemed surprised and relieved as she dug out her ticket stub, but as soon as I said '23B' it became obvious that she didn't understand enough English to translate my words into a seat on the plane. So I picked up a couple of her bags that had fallen on the floor and motioned for her to follow me. I helped her stow away her luggage and take off her coat, and I made sure she got buckled in to 23B. Then I returned to my seat.

May I be mystical for a moment? When I sat down in my seat, a wave of warmth and well-being flowed through me. The frustration and anxiety that had so filled me for most of the day started to dissipate. I felt like my parched, dusty soul had just been washed by a warm summer rain. For the first time in almost eighteen hours, I felt good.

What Proverbs 11:17 says is true. Our souls are nourished when we are kind. That's not the only reason for doing good, but it's an undeniable benefit. Generally speaking, when we do good, we feel good.

That doesn't mean we feel smug or proud or self-righteous; it means that we experience that calm and quiet – and humbling – inner awareness that we have just had the privilege of being a channel of God's love.

Even children can experience this. I remember one winter when my children were young and we had a huge snowstorm. We were out clearing our drive when I noticed that the drive of our neighbours, who were going through a difficult time, had not been cleared. So, after we had cleared our drive, I dragged the children and their miniature shovels next door, and we started clearing the neighbours' drive. At first the children were moaning and complaining about missing their favourite television programme, but by the time we neared the end of the drive, they had got into the spirit of the task and were working cheerfully. That night, when I tucked them into their beds in their separate rooms, they each talked about how good it felt to help someone else.

In a snowstorm on a weekday evening my children learned what many of the Willow Creek congregation learn during a weekend in Chicago on what we call Urban Plunges. On Saturday mornings they meet in the church car park, pile into vans and drive into inner city areas to work with some of our church's partners in ministry. Often when I come to church late on Saturday afternoons to prepare for our evening service, I run into people just returning from their Urban Plunge. They are usually standing around in little groups saying, 'You know, I've never worked so hard in my life – and I've never felt so good!'

Why do we feel good when we do good? The main reason is that we are made in the image of a God who is by nature good. That means that he, and therefore we, have an enormous capacity for doing good – great potential for goodness – and we naturally delight in doing good. Each time we live up to that potential, God himself smiles and says, 'Ah, that's exactly what I hoped you would do.' We sense that smile and those words as an inner affirmation of who we are and what we have done.

'For we are God's workmanship,' writes Paul in Ephesians 2:10, 'created in Christ Jesus to do good works, which God prepared in advance for us to do.' Can it be any clearer? We were created to do good works. When we do them we fulfil our purpose in being alive. We take hold of our destiny as human beings. Though our good works may at times require great sacrifices of time, money or energy, we can also do good through such simple acts as communicating kindness through our eyes, speaking a gracious word or offering an appropriate touch. But however simple or dramatic our acts of goodness, the point is that goodness is to become a way of life for us who are made in the image of God. When it does, our good deeds will not only help others but also nourish our own souls.

Those who deserve it

I suppose I could end this chapter here and say, 'Get on with it. Take hold of your destiny by doing good. Respond to your calling with random acts of kindness. Give expression to the image of God by helping others. Just do it!' But I believe that would be irresponsible. Do good? Yes, of course. But how? When? Where? To whom? How often? Are we called to offer goodness indiscriminately? To anyone, at any time? To everyone, every time? What does the Bible say?

The truth is, there is more to living in the image of God than indiscriminately performing good deeds. Being finite human beings, we have limited resources of time and energy; we can't respond to every need in the universe. Committing random acts of kindness may be a nice idea and a catchy slogan for mugs and car stickers, but in reality we may have to apply a little thoughtful strategy to our doing of good deeds.

The Bible helps us do this by qualifying the command to do good deeds. We discover the first qualification in Proverbs 3:27, which says, 'Do not withhold good from those who deserve it, when it is in your power to act.' When the wise writer of this proverb tells us to do good to those who deserve it, he implies that there are some people who may not deserve it.

One clear example of a group of people who didn't deserve the acts of goodness they hoped to receive is recorded in the second letter the apostle Paul wrote to the Christians in the town of Thessalonica. In the first century, a community of believers in that city established a food bank to feed those who were unable to work and provide for themselves. However, some able-bodied men and women saw the food bank as the way to an easy life. So they left their jobs and began to live off the goodness of the responsible, hard-working, compassionate believers who had stocked the shelves. In response to this problem, Paul wrote these words:

> In the name of the Lord Jesus Christ, we command you, brothers, to keep away from every brother who is idle and does not live according to the teaching you received from us. For you yourselves know how you ought to follow our example. We were not idle when we were with you, nor did we eat anyone's food without paying for it. On the contrary, we worked night and day, labouring and toiling so that we would not be a burden to any of you. We did this, not because we do not have the right to such help, but in order to make ourselves a model for you to follow. For even when we were with you, we gave you this rule: 'If a man will not work, he shall not eat.'
>
> We hear that some among you are idle. They are not busy; they are busybodies. Such people we command and urge in the Lord Jesus Christ to settle down and earn the bread they eat. And as for you, brothers, never tire of doing what is right.
>
> If anyone does not obey our instruction in this letter, take special note of him. Do not associate with him, in order that he may feel ashamed. Yet do not regard him as an enemy, but warn him as a brother. (2 Thessalonians 3:6–15)

This is the kind of passage I like to read to people who say that the Bible is 'so confusing'. Is there any doubt what Paul meant in this passage? Is there any doubt of how he felt about people who should have been working and buying their own food but who chose instead to waste their time in idleness and gossip and in working out clever ways to sponge off the goodness of others?

Proverbs 3:27, the verse we began with, makes it clear that some poor people really do need help, and we are called to help them. There is no doubt about that calling. But the Bible also teaches in the clearest terms that those who try to take advantage of goodness don't deserve it. God tells us not to waste our limited supply of goodness on conniving people who are trying to avoid taking personal responsibility for their lives. According to the Bible, such people should be warned as fellow-believers and made to 'feel ashamed'.

A help or a hindrance?

From Proverbs 16:26 we get a second qualification of the command to do good deeds. This verse says, 'The labourer's appetite works for him; his hunger drives him on.' In other words, hunger and other kinds of personal need or desire can be good for us, because they stimulate us to work diligently and provide for ourselves. What follows from this is that any acts of goodness that diminish the recipients' drive to work hard and meet their own needs are misspent goodness. It undermines people's development as responsible human beings and creates in them an unhealthy dependence on others.

For years this issue has been at the heart of heated debates about the welfare system and charitable gifts. As a council member for an international Christian relief organization, I have frequently been part of the difficult discussions surrounding relief. The organization I serve exists to help those who truly deserve and need intervention; to that end, it distributes hundreds of planeloads of food each year to impoverished and disaster-stricken regions of the world.

But what do we do when local farmers decide that rather than ploughing their fields and planting seeds and harvesting crops, they'll wait for the planes to come along? We can't afford to make mistakes about this. If necessary intervention crosses a fine line and creates an unhealthy dependence, a well-intentioned airlift of supplies could undermine an entire local economy. In this case, it takes sociological and economic understanding, plus spiritual discernment, to decide on ways of doing good that do not create unhealthy dependence.

Less complex but similarly damaging is the dependence that can be created between parents and children. When parents provide too freely for their children's material needs and wants, thereby satisfying their every desire, they discourage their children from working.

Well-meaning parents who leave large sums to their children do so believing that their generous provision will free their children to make noble choices and pursue worthwhile goals. Sometimes this happens. Too often, however, these good intentions seem to do children more harm than good; young people who have never been forced to learn the lessons taught by hard work tend to drift into self-indulgent lifestyles and often squander their gifts and opportunities.

It is good for parents to be able to assist their children financially; I look forward to helping my children financially as they pursue their education, begin their careers, and marry and start families (if God so leads them). But parents must not allow such help to foster irresponsibility in their children.

When my daughter, Shauna, was eleven, she got a part-time summer job in a beachwear shop owned by a friend of mine. At thirteen, my son, Todd, got a job washing boats at a little marina. I wanted both my children to learn at an early age what it feels like to work hard, to meet the standards of a boss, to earn money, to pay for items they need or want and to enjoy a satisfying sense of independence. I believe that such experiences have increased my children's ability to live responsibly during their years as young adults and will serve them well throughout their lives.

Exchanging favours

A third qualification of the command to do good comes from the lips of Jesus. 'Then Jesus said to his host, "When you give a luncheon or dinner, do not invite your friends, your brothers or relatives, or your rich neighbours; if you do, they may invite you back and so you will be repaid. But when you give a banquet, invite the poor, the crippled, the lame, the blind, and you will be blessed. Although they cannot repay you, you will be repaid at the resurrection of the righteous"' (Luke 14:12–14).

Jesus' concern in this passage is about self-ingratiating acts of goodness, or good works done primarily in the hope of receiving something in return. He knows how easily we deceive ourselves about why we do what we do. He knows how quick we are to pat ourselves on the back for a selfless good deed when in reality we're just exchanging favours which have little if anything to do with true goodness.

It happens all the time in my community. People with huge homes invite other affluent people to extravagant dinners with the clear hope that the favour will be returned. Usually it is, and the practice of exchanging favours continues. There's nothing wrong with having such dinner parties, but they have little to do with true goodness.

Just down the road from my church is a residential centre for mentally handicapped adults. According to Jesus, a 'true-goodness' dinner party might involve collecting four or five such residents and serving them a lovely dinner in one's own home. Or it might mean taking senior citizens from a nursing home to a community event and then out for a meal at a local restaurant. Another idea is to have a party or plan an outing for a group of physically or mentally disabled children. Imagine a dinner party that nourishes your own heart, as well as the bodies and hearts of children who all too often find themselves among the most neglected in our society. Many churches and communities have projects through which caring adults and families can provide hospitality, friendship or a simple conversation to those who could never return the favour.

We live in an extremely social culture. Whether we are senior citizens, middle-aged, young adults or teenagers, most of us are involved in numerous social gatherings. We attend community events, parties and concerts. We meet our friends in restaurants and coffee houses and college rooms. We fritter away hours watching television and going to films and attending sporting events. Why not transform some of those hours and opportunities into settings for what Jesus would consider 'true-goodness' parties? All we would have to do is invite a few people outside the normal circle of our friends, a few people who don't usually get invited, a few people like the ones Jesus might invite.

Asking the hard questions

The Bible makes it clear that we need to be careful in how we do acts of goodness so we don't waste goodness on those who don't actually deserve it, create unhealthy dependence or contribute to the self-serving exchange of favours. In addition to these biblical qualifications, we need to sharpen our skills of discernment.

I heartily endorse the work of organizations whose goal is to share the resources of the privileged few with the many needy people who struggle for survival in the cities of the developed world and in the wretched hovels of the Third World. My church has poured large amounts of money and time into a variety of projects in partnership with World Vision, Habitat for Humanity and many other God-honouring organizations. We have sent money and volunteers into the inner city of Chicago, and to Mexico, the Dominican Republic, and elsewhere around the world. Such ministry endeavours provide caring individuals with the opportunity to do good in ways they could not do alone. I believe that both individual believers and churches should take advantage of these opportunities.

But we must be discerning. We must ask hard questions of any individual or group to whom we are considering giving our time or money. Does this organization do exactly what it claims to do? Good intentions and impressive goals are not enough. Are the goals being achieved efficiently, effectively and honourably? Is the organization responsible in its use of money? Are audited accounts available? Are salaries justified?

In addition to asking these questions, we need to seek the Holy Spirit's confirmation. When we bring a particular form of ministry or good deed before God in prayer, do we have that personal inner sense that God affirms both the organization and our involvement with it? If we do, then the Bible would say to you and to me. 'Go for it! Don't hold back! Shower the work with your goodness. Encourage, serve, pray, give, volunteer as much time and energy as you can. Let the goodness flow like a mighty river.' But if we have any reservations, we mustn't be naive. Our resources of time, energy and money are limited; we mustn't throw them away on unworthy causes or ineffective efforts.

Do not withhold it

Do these warnings discourage you? Do you feel more motivated not to do good than to do it? Then look again at Proverbs 3:27: 'Do not withhold good from those who deserve it, when it is in your power to act.' In the previous pages I turned the verse inside out in order to deal with some negative qualifications and implications. But the main point of the verse is in the first four words: 'Do not withhold good.' In other words, we must not shrink back, chicken out, be lazy or turn the other way when the opportunity to do good comes our way. If the Spirit endorses it and it is in our power to do, we need to do it.

As I said before, we are made in the image of a God who is lavish in doing goodness, a God who delights in redeeming, restoring, refreshing, rebuilding and revitalizing. We need to remind ourselves of that every day and then remind ourselves that God has called us to do the same. Imagine how our world would be transformed if the some two billion people in the world who call themselves Christians were doing the goodness they have the power to do. Imagine what would happen if they were allowing God to do his work of loving and healing and encouraging through them. Take it a step further and imagine living in a world where all six or seven billion people were doing that.

Why don't we live in a world like that? Because the world is full of people like you and me who don't let the call to goodness penetrate our hearts and minds and souls and mouths and hands and feet.

Every time I fail to do an act of goodness that is in my power to do, I miss an important opportunity. And that particular opportunity is never available again. I will never again have the opportunity to help the needy, Los Angeles-bound woman I described at the beginning of this chapter. What if I hadn't been preparing a sermon on Proverbs that week? What if I hadn't been reminded as I worked on that sermon that my own soul would be nourished if I was kind to someone else? What if the deep-rooted selfishness of my own heart hadn't been overruled for just a minute by the challenge of God's word? I don't know the answers to those questions. Maybe someone else would have helped that woman. Maybe not.

It may well be that the vast majority of unfulfilled needs that bring sadness, heartache, loneliness and despair into human lives are merely the results of good deeds left undone. Think about that. Think about the incredible power of good deeds; think about the tragedy of our failure to do them. The book of Proverbs tells us that when it comes to good deeds, God and others are relying on us. If it is in our power to do good, we had better do it.

Never enough

But what if it is not in our power? In calling us to do good 'when it is in our power to do it', this proverb implies that there may be times when it is not in our power to do a specific good deed. Though we earnestly desire to respond to a given need, we lack the knowledge, the skill, the opportunity, the time, the talent, the resources or the energy required to do so.

When that is really true, the book of Proverbs tells us not to condemn ourselves or to slip into despair because we think we are failing a needy world. At such times we must say tenderly but firmly, 'It is not in my power to do that.' Then we need to trust God to assign that particular task to someone else.

I mention this because I know many sensitive, good-hearted people who live with a 'never-enough' cloud hanging over their heads. Though their hearts are filled with the goodness of God and they willingly pour themselves out in acts of goodness for others, they never sense the smile of God or experience the nourishment of their own souls, because thirty seconds after completing one good deed they start condemning themselves for not doing more. They are unable to detach themselves from the needs they see around them, and they have slipped into a spiral of despair. They have become so consumed with the sadness of our sin-stained world that they have lost touch with the simple joys of being alive. They have become so aware of the darkness of our weary planet they have lost sight of its many brilliant reflections of divine beauty and light. They have become so sensitive to the various griefs and losses of humanity that they have forgotten why and how to celebrate. Day in and day out they live under the grey, brooding cloud of 'never enough'.

To these people the book of Proverbs says in essence, 'Your God is a huge God with unlimited resources. The family of God is a huge family with many people to share the responsibility for doing good. You need to learn to assume the responsibilities that are yours and let go of those that aren't. When it is in your power to do good, do it. When it is not in your power to do it, then breathe a genuine prayer of concern and intercession and ask God to provide someone else to meet that need.'

What I'm talking about here is the issue of boundaries, which in recent years has been the subject of many fine Christian books. In a community of believers in which too many of us have been taught to give everything we have, to sacrifice all for the cause and never to think of our own welfare, this issue requires thoughtful clarification and an earnest pursuit of the guidance of the Holy Spirit. Though this chapter does not provide the context for an in-depth treatment of this subject, I would like to draw from the Bible a few observations about what I call 'boundaried' goodness.

No more and no less

The most famous biblical parable about doing good is probably the parable of the good Samaritan recorded in Luke 10:25–37. You've undoubtedly heard the story. A Samaritan picked up a man who had been beaten up by robbers and left for dead along the roadside. The Samaritan cleaned and bandaged the man's wounds, put him on his own donkey and took him to an inn where he could be cared for. He paid the innkeeper in advance for the wounded man's care but promised that on his return trip he would stop and pay any additional expenses that might be incurred while the man was recuperating.

Jesus commended the Samaritan's good deed and commanded his followers to do likewise. Ever since Jesus first told that story it has been used effectively to motivate Christians and non-Christians alike to do tangible acts of compassion and kindness. But it is not a call to indiscriminate goodness. The Samaritan did a great deal for the wounded man; he literally soiled his hands with the blood of the man's wounds, and he wrote a virtually blank cheque to pay for the man's care. But there are some important things the Samaritan didn't do.

While he did take the man to an inn, he didn't cancel his trip in order to care for him. Perhaps it was a business trip, and he knew his boss was counting on him to get a new customer or satisfy a client. Or maybe the trip was a family responsibility that he rightly deemed a higher priority than anything else that week. At any rate, he continued on his journey.

We can assume that the Samaritan returned to the inn and paid the man's bill, as he had promised to do, but Scripture gives no indication that he did anything more to help the man. He didn't take the man home with him to continue his recuperation. We don't read that he treated him like a son for the rest of his life or gave him part of his inheritance. We have no indication that he continued his relationship with the man in any way.

What did he do? He did the good that he had the power to do in the manner the Holy Spirit led him to do it. The book of Proverbs calls us to do the same: to do the acts of goodness we have the power to do in the manner in which the Holy Spirit leads us to do them. No more and no less. When we do that, our goodness flows joyfully and leaves us free to respond with kindness and compassion to the next genuine need we see.

Caring in community

Some churches, including Willow Creek, have a food bank open to people from the church or the community who are going through times of desperate need. Twice a year our church restocks the shelves of the food bank at our weekend services. The last time we did this, an older, well-dressed woman approached me after a service and said, 'I started attending this church five years ago. Shortly after that I became a

Christian, and for several years my life was going really well. I loved being able to fill my boot with bags of groceries for the food bank.' Then her lip began to tremble, and she continued in a whisper, 'But my circumstances have changed . . . I can't bring even a single bag . . . I had to go to the food bank myself . . .'

I put my arm around her shoulder while she cried. 'The beauty of the church', I told her, 'is that those of us whose lives are going well and who have money to spare are called by the Spirit of God to give to others graciously and generously, as you have done many times in the past. At the same time, those who are faced with a genuine need are called by the Spirit to receive from others with a spirit of thankfulness, as you are doing now. Those who give do so with the humble realization that one unforeseen change in circumstances could throw them into a position of desperate need. Those who receive do so with the prayer that in time they will be blessed with abundance from which to give. That's part of what it means to live in fellowship with others in a community of faith.'

Many years ago, that view of Christian community led a group of car mechanics to start a Willow Creek project called CARS. They devised a plan to set up garage in the church maintenance building and mend the cars of single mothers who couldn't afford the necessary repairs. They agreed to volunteer their time and expertise if the church would pay for parts. The ministry expanded as church members who were getting new cars and didn't need to sell their old one began donating their used cars to the church.

CARS volunteers cleaned and repaired these cars and began giving them to women whose cars were no longer worth repairing or to other people who desperately needed transport. In one recent year six hundred vehicles were donated to the CARS ministry. Some were sold for parts, but most were refurbished and given to legitimately needy people.

One family that donated a car left an assortment of papers on the dashboard – gift vouchers for our church bookshop and café, coupons for five free car washes and five free oil changes and a note that read, 'You have no idea how much joy it is for our family to pass this blessing on to you.' How well served was the person or family who received that car? How nourished was the collective soul of the family that gave it? How alive was the Spirit of Christ in the life of our church community? That's what acts of goodness do. They honour and encourage everyone involved.

Doing good in community also allows us to achieve far more than we ever could on our own. It also spreads the burden and responsibility so individuals do not have to become exhausted by doing good.

The ultimate act of goodness

While we are commanded by God to respond to the tangible needs of others with practical acts of care and compassion, there is an even greater good we can offer to others: an introduction to the God of the universe. What more pressing burden does any man or woman carry than the burden of separation from God through sin? What deeper need does a person have than to be reconciled to God through Christ? If we can help people understand the divine love manifested in the substitutionary death of Christ and the divine power manifested in the resurrection of Christ, we will have given them the ultimate gift.

Several years ago I helped a friend establish a relationship with God. One of the great joys of my life was the telephone call in which he informed me that he finally understood the gospel of grace and that he had just accepted Christ as his Saviour. Last year, on the second anniversary of that day, he wrote me a note that said, 'Dear Bill, I'm two years new today. Two years ago when I was lost, the words *amazing grace* meant nothing to me, but now that I've been found, they mean the world to me. Thank you for everything.' In the letter he underlined the word *everything* repeatedly, because he knew that in becoming a Christian he received everything he needed: forgiveness of sin, cleansing of his conscience, adoption into the family of God, hope for the future, purpose in life and the promise of heaven.

Do you really want to do good? Then commit yourself to doing every tangible act of goodness that the Holy Spirit leads you to do and also live with the daily awareness that if you introduce someone to God, you will have given that person the greatest gift of goodness you can give.

The memory bank of heaven
Throughout this chapter I have mixed challenges with warnings, and promptings with qualifications. The necessary call to establish healthy boundaries must be balanced by the equally necessary call to

perform faithful acts of service to others over a long period. Galatians 6:9 has been the motto for my ministry for over two decades. It says, 'Let us not become weary in doing good, for at the proper time we will reap a harvest if we do not give up.'

One of the biggest hindrances to doing good over a long period is the discouragement that often sets in when we see little positive impact from our efforts or see the world getting darker and sadder and more lost despite our hard work. 'What's the use?' we ask. 'Why should I keep on doing my little part? Why should I bother to care? What good does it do?'

The temptation is to move from discouragement to cynicism to self-absorption. People who used to overflow with love and be active in good works begin withdrawing into the small world of self-protection and isolation. Given the heartaches and disappointments they have known, they believe withdrawal is justified; they think they are doing themselves a favour. But as their external worlds get smaller, their inner worlds shrivel too. In turning their backs on the needs around them they have turned their backs on the needs of their own souls.

There are several antidotes to discouragement and cynicism besides closing one's heart to the needy and withdrawing into a shrunken world filled only with one's own concerns. One antidote to weariness in doing good is to pay attention to the warnings and qualifications outlined in this chapter. That means learning to balance compassion with discernment and selfless giving with the mental discipline to say, 'This is as far as God has called me to go.'

Another antidote is to walk closely with the One

who alone can fill our hearts with goodness. It is necessary for those of us committed to doing good to allow ourselves to be refreshed and renewed in the quiet presence of God on a regular basis.

One reason for the biblical command to honour the sabbath day is that we all need time to rest from responsibilities and to receive spiritual and emotional nourishment. We need a weekly reminder that we are as accepted and loved by God when we sit quietly and restfully in his presence as we are when we are actively doing good for his sake. We need a weekly reminder that God is at work through our efforts in ways we can't yet see, and if we could see them we would probably have cause for hope, even celebration. We need a weekly reminder that we are just a small part in God's process of loving and redeeming his creation and that he doesn't expect us to carry the cares of his world on our frail shoulders. We need a weekly reminder that sometimes our earnest and faithful prayers are the greatest good works we can offer to others.

In addition to accepting the spiritual refreshments of the sabbath rest, we need to give ourselves the freedom to enjoy God-given pleasures. We need to take the time to open our senses to the invigorating beauty of nature or music or art. We need to let ourselves receive the gifts of good food, good friends or good books. We need to create time and space in our lives for whatever specific means God uses to refresh us, whether that be gardening or walking on the beach or sailing boats or painting pictures or running marathons. If our lives feel like constant drudgery we are probably not listening to that whisper of the Spirit that calls us to rest and refresh ourselves.

I've learned from experience, and probably you have too, that it is easy to lose heart in doing good. That is why we all need to commit ourselves to establishing necessary boundaries and creating a healthy balance in our lives. Only then can we be faithful conduits of God's goodness until the day we die.

That truly is a challenging goal – to be faithful conduits of God's goodness – but it is a goal that comes with the promise of reward. One of the most moving biblical passages regarding this reward is the words Jesus himself will say to his followers when he greets them in heaven. Matthew 25:34–40 says:

> Then the King will say to those on his right, 'Come, you who are blessed by my Father; take your inheritance, the kingdom prepared for you since the creation of the world. For I was hungry and you gave me something to eat, I was thirsty and you gave me something to drink, I was a stranger and you invited me in, I needed clothes and you clothed me, I was sick and you looked after me, I was in prison and you came to visit me.'
>
> Then the righteous will answer him, 'Lord, when did we see you hungry and feed you or thirsty and give you something to drink? When did we see you a stranger and invite you in, or needing clothes and clothe you? When did we see you sick or in prison and go to visit you?'
>
> The King will reply, 'I tell you the truth, whatever you did for one of the least of these brothers of mine, you did for me.'

In the economy of God, whenever we do good to anybody – a lonely widow in a nursing home, a penitent inmate of a local prison, a hungry child in a Third-World orphanage, a struggling single mother in a suburban area, a weary shopper in a queue at the supermarket checkout, a lonely student lamenting his parents' divorce – whenever we do good for anyone like these, it's as if we are doing it for Christ himself, and our act of goodness so penetrates his soul that it becomes permanently etched in the memory bank of heaven.

4
Develop discipline

When my children were young I used to read them a book that was a word-association quiz. I read the description of a person who worked in a particular profession, and the children had to name the most important tool that person would use in his or her work. I'd read about a carpenter, and the children would shout out *hammer*. I'd read about a dentist, and they'd mumble *drill*. For a surgeon, the word would be *scalpel*. For a drummer, *drumstick*. For a bricklayer, *trowel*. For a seamstress, *needle*. For an astronomer, *telescope*. For a referee, *whistle*. For a writer, *pen*. (Obviously the book was written before the day of word processors, when writers still used pens.)

What was significant about each of these tools of the trade was that to the worker who used them, they were indispensable. Without a hammer the carpenter couldn't build a house. Without a scalpel the surgeon couldn't perform an operation. Without a telescope the astronomer couldn't see the stars.

When it comes to the work of living, Proverbs tells us that the most indispensable tool available to all of us is *discipline*. Without it we cannot live productive, satisfying lives. Proverbs 13:18 says, 'He who ignores discipline comes to poverty and shame.' While poverty and shame may manifest themselves in many forms, ignoring discipline always manifests itself in a life sliding towards ruin. If we fail to take discipline seriously, we do so at our own peril.

The notion of discipline often conjures up negative images involving punishment: we envisage a child being smacked, a soldier being shouted at or a student being expelled. Or we think of discipline as an unavoidable evil, as an oppressive pattern of rigid routines and daily deprivations, imposed on us by some outside force determined to make our lives miserable. According to this view, discipline is the enemy, the obvious foe of a happy, meaningful, joy-filled life.

But not everyone views discipline that way. I recently read an article about a woman who wins many wheelchair marathons. When she was asked how she manages to do well so consistently, she said that she disciplines herself to train in her wheelchair for one hundred miles each week. She sees this form of discipline as the only means of maintaining her competitive edge. It is the tool she uses to develop the strength and speed and endurance she wants to have. When she crosses the finishing line, do you think she views the discipline that got her there as an unavoidable evil?

Some time ago I was in a small aeroplane in horrible weather conditions. I watched as the pilot in command flew us through rain, wind shear, thunderstorms and hail and finally brought us to a safe landing. I have taken enough flying lessons to know that what enabled that pilot to bring us safely through such threatening weather conditions was the discipline of hundreds of hours spent in training classes, flight simulators and test flights with examiners – all to keep his skills sharp. Without that, there is no way he could have performed flawlessly under such adverse conditions. Our safety that night was the direct result of his unwavering commitment to discipline. Dare we call such discipline an enemy?

A friend of mine recently had major surgery. When I talked with him before he entered the hospital he assured me that there was nothing to worry about; the surgeon he had chosen had performed this procedure thirteen hundred times. In fact, he told me, people from all over the country wait weeks or even months to entrust themselves to this particular surgeon.

If we could ask that surgeon how he had built a national reputation for excellence and skill, I am sure he would describe to us years of studying late into the night, going on seemingly endless hospital rounds, examining hundreds of patients and practising routine procedures over and over again. He would probably say, 'It was hard. Incredibly hard. Ridiculously hard.' If we pressed him further and asked what kept him going through it all, he might well answer with one word: *discipline*. If we asked him whether the discipline that kept him relentlessly pursuing his goals was a friend or a foe, I am confident that he would claim discipline was his dearest friend. Why? Because it has allowed him to achieve something of great significance that matters deeply to him.

We must learn to view discipline as an indispensable tool for making life work and as our greatest asset when it comes to achieving our goals. But in order to use the tool we need to understand it. In this chapter I want to take some of the mystery out of discipline by breaking it down and looking at its various components. This will help us to apply discipline more effectively in our lives.

Aim high

The first component of discipline is the establishment of a high goal. If this surprises you, ask yourself this question: Why develop discipline if we don't have a goal challenging enough to require discipline? Why pay the price if it is not necessary? If we are aiming for nothing more than a minimally challenging job, a few casual relationships or a passable spiritual life, there is little reason to develop or sharpen this tool of discipline. There is no need to bother with discipline if we can meander through life without it.

But if our goals are loftier than that, then discipline becomes a necessity. If we dream of fulfilling our highest potential in our education and our work, we need discipline. If we dream of being a spouse, a parent or a friend who breathes life into other people, we need discipline. If we dream of honouring God in our finances and serving others with our money, we need discipline. If we dream of using our spiritual gifts in a meaningful way, we need discipline. If we dream of maintaining our physical health through our diet and exercise, we need discipline.

Every accomplished doctor, lawyer, musician, actor, writer, athlete, salesperson, business leader, teacher, craftsman, speaker, sailor, racing car driver, shopkeeper – in short, every accomplished worker I know in any field – has tapped into the power of discipline for the simple reason that he or she had to. Those people could not get where they wanted to go without it.

I know that some people get a bit squeamish about dreaming big dreams; they are afraid that setting lofty goals is presumptuous or arrogant. But what is presumptuous or arrogant about desiring to learn and grow and achieve? Part of what it means to be made in the image of God is that we aspire to make a significant difference with our lives and to fulfil all the potential that has been entrusted to us. We should never apologize for that.

It will take tremendous effort to pursue those dreams and reach those goals. But what a reward when we begin to see the fruits of our effort. Proverbs 13:12 says that 'a longing fulfilled is a tree of life'. A strong desire to grow comes from God. When we work hard and eventually fulfil that desire, we receive a reward that is invigorating and beautiful, like a tree of life.

I don't know about you, but one day I hope to be sitting in a deckchair in my back garden (or maybe riding a motorcycle up and down the path), looking back over the years and saying, 'What a gift it was to be able to work and strive and discipline myself to reach the goals God put in my heart. Those were great days!'

Throughout human history, popular thought has weighed the value of leisure against that of work. Current thought swings between the opposing views of those who so exalt the work ethic that they sacrifice nearly everything else to achieve their goals and those who unapologetically flaunt their disdain of hard work and accomplishment. Can we avoid those two extremes and wholeheartedly agree that setting a broad range of high goals under the umbrella of God's guidance is a necessary step on the path towards a meaningful life?

What about you? Are your current goals high enough to move you along that path? Are they high enough to demand the development of discipline?

Pay now, play later

The next component, which is at the core of discipline, is delayed gratification. M. Scott Peck in his book *The Road Less Travelled* defines *delayed gratification* as nothing more than arranging the pains and the pleasures of life in such a way as to secure and improve the season of pleasure by facing the pain first and getting it over with.

For a developmental view of how delayed gratification works, imagine a three-year-old at his birthday party with a huge piece of chocolate cake staring up at him from the middle of his plastic plate. Manifesting wisdom (and words) well beyond his years, the little fellow says to himself, 'In order to make this experience the best that it can be, I'm going to exercise discipline. I'm going to apply the principle of delayed gratification.' What does he do? He fills his little hand with cake and crams it into his mouth. Then again. And again. Finally, all that is left is a giant sticky mound of chocolate icing. Smiling to himself, he prepares for the next part of his culinary experience by taking a few deep breaths. Then he scoops and licks and swallows, again and again, congratulating himself on saving the best (the icing) until last. *Ah*, he thinks, *life doesn't get any better than this*.

A couple of years later the little fellow goes to school and discovers that the same principle applies to doing homework. If he tackles and completes his work straight after school, he can then play football with his friends until his mother calls him in for dinner. After dinner he can play with his brothers and sisters all evening, and in the morning there's no panic over the homework. He hates that period of studying straight after school, but it is worth it not to have the homework hanging over his head for the rest of the evening. He's a pretty bright child, isn't he?

He applies the same principle throughout his school years, and after graduating from college he accepts a junior position in a company. It is not the job of his dreams, and it requires long hours and hard work, but he considers it as an investment for the future. He hopes that if he goes the extra mile and pays the price during his early working years, he will enjoy an extended time of reward later on. His plan pays off. Twenty years later he is the head of his department and second in line for a directorship.

He is also enjoying a level of financial security that many of his peers can only dream of. Why? Because years ago he made some difficult choices regarding his budget. First, in line with the teaching of Scripture, he decided to support the redemptive purposes of God by offering to God a tenth of what he earned each month. Secondly, he decided to invest regularly in a savings fund, and he enrolled in his company's profit-sharing scheme. Working diligently and living within his means has allowed him to reach middle age with minimal debts and no major financial burdens weighing him down. He looks forward to his retirement, knowing that his profit-sharing scheme and his personal investments will allow him and his wife to enjoy their old age. Not a bad life, is it?

Of course the principle of delayed gratification is no guarantee that life will work out the way it seems to be working for our imaginary friend. We human beings don't have ultimate control over the course of our lives; we live in a world in which the realities of sin and suffering often take us down paths we neither anticipate nor choose. Still, delayed gratification is the best means we have of living responsibly and honourably before God and of finding meaning and joy in whatever life brings to us. This is true in every dimension of life.

Consider the area of relationships. You begin to build a new friendship and it is going well; you grow very fond of the other person, and the feeling seems to be mutual. But then you have a disagreement that proves difficult to resolve, and you both end up withdrawing into silence. Now you have a decision to make. Will you call that person and try to work out the conflict? Or will you let the friendship slowly die? You know it will be an extremely difficult and risky conversation; you know there is no guarantee that the other person will respond positively to your attempts at reconciliation. You may not even be sure you want him or her to do so. Why the work and the pain? Why endure this difficult relationship when it would be far easier to give up and find a new friend?

Why? Because the principle of delayed gratification tells you that if you initiate a reconciliation now, you may well receive a wonderful reward in the future. So you make the telephone call. You say, 'I know this is going to be a difficult conversation. But I think we have to talk. If we can face this painful issue and work it through, maybe we can re-establish our friendship and enjoy it for the rest of our lives. How about it?' If the other person accepts your olive branch and the conflict is resolved, this temporarily painful time can lead to a lifetime of pleasure. How many failed relationships might have been saved if the people involved had been willing to endure the challenges of resolving conflicts for the sake of future peace?

Another area of life in which the principle of delayed gratification plays an essential role is the area of physical fitness. It is not easy to run three miles every day, to take a long walk or to lift weights regularly. I have been doing such things for twenty years, and almost every day, when I put on my running shoes, I think to myself, 'I don't feel like doing this.' But every time I complete my run or my weight-lifting routine, I am reminded that 'it's fun when it's done'. And when I realize that I have more energy and a greater sense of physical well-being today than I had twenty years ago, I am grateful that I was taught at an early age that putting pain before pleasure is a good way to get a worthwhile reward.

Again, this principle of delayed gratification is at the heart of discipline. That is not to say it is easy; on the contrary, it is extremely difficult to deny ourselves now for the sake of a later reward. Hebrews 12:11 says, 'No discipline seems pleasant at the time, but painful.' This passage is primarily about the discipline of God, but it applies to other forms of discipline as well, and there is not one disciplined person who would deny the truth of it; discipline in any form is painful. But the verse continues with these words: 'Later on, however, it [discipline] produces a harvest of righteousness and peace for those who have been trained by it.' The pain is inevitable, but so is the harvest, the reward.

One final thought on delayed gratification: it is not an ability given only to some. Some people claim they are incapable of developing this component of discipline, but the truth is that we can all make progress in this area if we want to. We can all learn to save the icing until last!

Decide now

The third component of discipline takes us into the 18-certificate section of the book of Proverbs, into the early chapters concerning the folly of sexual sin. Though human sexuality is the backdrop for this particular discussion, the principle of discipline it highlights can be broadly applied, as you will see. I call this third component the principle of advance decision-making.

Look with me at Proverbs 5:7–8, in which the author is warning his sons about a loose woman who lives down the road. He says, 'Now then, my sons, listen to me; do not turn aside from what I say. Keep to a path far from her, do not go near the door of her house.' In verse after verse in the early chapters of Proverbs the authors write some variation on this theme: if you want to avoid sexual sin, you need to decide in advance to avoid sexual temptations. In this passage, the father says in essence, 'Listen to me. I have a plan for you. Don't go near the loose woman's house. Don't walk down her street. Decide now that you won't go there. Then stick to the plan. Don't waver.'

I can imagine this father taking his discussion a step further. 'Make your decision now, my sons, in broad daylight, while your thinking is clear and your mind is in control of your body. Consider the consequences of your actions. Look both at the benefits of sexual purity and at the high costs of sexual sin. Consider the value of having a clean conscience before God. Consider the value of maintaining your integrity before your friends. Consider the value of not having to worry about sexually transmitted diseases and unwanted pregnancies.'

To a married son he would add, 'Consider the value of honouring your marriage vows. Consider the value of maintaining your integrity before your children.' To all his sons he would say, 'Now consider the alternative. Reflect on what sexual sin could do to your relationship with God, to the important people in your life, to your body, to your future. Then make a wise decision and stick to it. Commit yourself to it before God and before a few trusted friends who will agree to hold you accountable. Do this, my sons. Please.'

The guidance of this wise father amounts to a cost-benefit analysis. 'Weigh the alternatives,' he says. 'Compare the choices. Then, make the right decision – now.' I think this father knew that if his sons failed to decide in advance to avoid sexual temptation, they would probably yield to it eventually. What he said to them was, 'If you fail to think ahead, and you end up trying to make the right decision in the midst of a sexually tempting situation . . . you're toast!'

Toast? I know what you're thinking – that this sounds like something children would say. But I am not making this up; it is a Hebrew expression, straight from Proverbs 6:25–26. 'Do not lust in your heart after her beauty or let her captivate you with her eyes, for the prostitute reduces you to a loaf of bread.' The writers of these proverbs knew what they were talking about!

The point of all of this is that few people are strong enough to make morally heroic choices in the midst of powerful temptations. Most of us discover that our good judgment wavers when the pressure is on. Proverbs 6:27–28 says, 'Can a man scoop fire into his lap without his clothes being burned? Can a man walk on hot coals without his feet being scorched?'

We would all like to consider ourselves invulnerable to temptation and sin. But part of maturing is understanding and acknowledging our vulnerabilities. When we do that, we realize how important it is to make the critical decisions of our lives well in advance of the situations or circumstances that tend to play on our fears, our weaknesses, our unfulfilled needs or our impure desires. We each have an internal collection of these negative tendencies, and we each experience the external pushing and pulling of a morally bankrupt world. That means we will each struggle with our own unique set of vulnerabilities. But that does not mean we cannot live with integrity, as long as we are disciplined enough to make important decisions in the light of day when our thinking is clear.

A personal foundation

I have built my life on the principle of advance decision-making. Had I not, I probably would not be walking closely with God today. I am a little embarrassed to admit this, but the truth about me is that if I do not set aside a time for a private meeting with God at least once in every twenty-four hours, I tend to drift way off course spiritually. Instead of devoting myself to God's agenda, I become consumed with my own agenda. Instead of being sensitive to people around me, I become insensitive. Instead of trying to work out how to be a greater servant of my congregation, I start working out manipulative ways to get other people to do my bidding. And it only takes two or three days of missing meetings with God to put me in that serious condition.

So, many years ago I made an advance decision. I said, 'God, I need to meet with you when I am at my most alert and clear-thinking. Because I am a morning person, I'm going to set aside the earliest moments of my day to meet with you. I'm not going to ask myself if I feel like doing that. I'm just going to do it.'

That means that every morning when I get to my office at church I pour myself a cup of coffee, open my Bible and let the truth of God's word fill my spirit. Then I take out a pen and a spiral notebook, and I chronicle God's activity in my life during the previous day, so that I can be encouraged, challenged, chastened or edified. I also write out my prayers to God so that I don't lose concentration. Had I not made an advance decision to maintain that routine every morning, I am sure I would have stopped doing it long ago, and I would have missed out on an experience that God has used time and time again to redirect my thinking and reactivate my spirit. What I have just described to you has formed the foundation of my life and ministry.

I also use advance decision-making in sermon preparation. I once heard a business leader say that good leaders should give their best hours to the most significant contributions they are called upon to make to their organization. Although writing sermons is by far the hardest thing I do, it is one of my major responsibilities as senior pastor. Though I am as prone as anyone else to avoid unpleasant or difficult tasks, I have discovered that church services come around with amazing regularity, and when they arrive I need to have a sermon written and ready to deliver. What that means is that for the past twenty years I have had to block out the hours from 6.30 a.m. to 10.30 or 11 a.m., five days a week, in order to read the Bible, pray and write out sermons.

When people invite me out for breakfast, I have to turn them down (even those who appeal to my Dutch thriftiness and offer to pay the bill!). Staff members at my church have given up trying to get me to attend a morning meeting. I know that unless I make an advance decision and stick to it, I won't be able to do what God has called me to do in my teaching ministry.

Advance decision-making has also made a huge difference in my parenting. When my children were young, I knew that unless I was at home four nights a week, no matter what was going on at church, I was going to undermine my relationship with them. I am not saying that four nights per week is the magic number for every family, but as I looked at *my* children in *our* family, I concluded that as the father I needed to be present four nights a week. The only way I could do that was to discipline myself to get out my calendar a year in advance and write 'home night, home night, home night, home night'. When I was away during a given week I made sure I spent additional time with the children the following week, and frequently I took one child or the other on trips with me, in order to create special one-to-one memories.

But I had to make these scheduling commitments and decisions in advance. Had I tried to make them at the last minute, while I sorted through a pile of important issues and invitations to speak, there is no way I would have set aside adequate time for Shauna and Todd – and I would not have the precious relationships I have with them today.

Another implication that advance decision-making had on my parenting practices was that I began teaching my children, while they were still very young, the biblical values upon which moral decisions and character development are based. I also began involving them in decision-making at an early age, gradually teaching them how to do cost-benefit analyses of increasingly complex issues.

I have never agreed with the *laissez-faire* approach to childrearing in which parents allow their children almost unhindered freedom to 'unfold and develop' on their own. I believe this does a great disservice to children and that it has left many young people today without a foundation for the decision-making aspects of discipline. It seems to me that wise parents should offer wise decision-making guidance along the way, so that by the time their children reach their teenage years, they will already have made many important decisions about what to do when they face various challenges and temptations – and they will probably achieve a far higher moral standard than children do who enter those years unprepared.

Let me say it again

If you are starting to get the idea that I don't want to leave the subject of advance decision-making, you're right. I know how critical it has been in my life, and I keep wondering if I'm making the point strongly enough. Am I? Are you getting the message? Do you see the implications it could have for your relationship with God, for your family life, for your work, for your ministry, for the way you care for your body?

Consider a little thing like getting up in the morning. Do you wish you had an extra half-hour before you left for work or school so you could pray or plan your day or have breakfast with your family? If you were going to apply the principle of advance decision-making, you would set your alarm clock half an hour earlier, and while you were setting it, you would say, 'When this thing goes off tomorrow morning, I am getting up. I am not going to lie in bed analysing my biorhythms and asking myself whether or not I feel like getting up. I don't care how I feel. I am going to get up when the alarm goes off because that is what I have decided to do. It is the right decision, and I am going to stick to it.' Then in the morning, the principle of advance decision-making kicks you out of bed and gets you to start your day on the right foot.

Or consider something bigger, like building meaningful friendships. I often hear people complain that they don't have any close friends, but that is usually because they have failed to take disciplined action to establish such relationships. A disciplined person would say, 'I am going to make a major decision to get involved in a small group of fellow Christians where other people will be looking for friends too, and I am going to act on that decision. Then, every time the group meets, I am going to turn up and be open and build some friendships.' In a year or eighteen months, that man or woman probably will be able to look around a dining-room table and see four or five people who have become like brothers and sisters – thanks to an advance decision.

Advance decision-making can also offer huge rewards when it comes to church attendance. The Bible speaks clearly about the discipline of Christians coming together in groups in order to help one another grow. Hebrews 10:25 says, 'Let us not give up meeting together, as some are in the habit of doing, but let us encourage one another.' Coming together, whether for formal church services or more informal small-group meetings, is not about following some legalistic rule; it is about taking advantage of a significant means of spiritual growth. You and I never know when God is going to turn up at a particular meeting of Christians in such a powerful and personal way that it touches our hearts and transforms us on the inside. If we take a casual approach to meeting together and say, 'It's raining outside today. I don't think I'll go to church,' we are risking missing out on what God wants to do in our lives.

After a recent service at Willow Creek a woman said to me, 'I could take you to the chair I was sitting on the day I first understood the message of amazing grace and opened my heart to Jesus Christ. Then I could take you to the chair I was sitting on when I decided to let go of a sinful habit that was destroying my life. I could take you to another chair where I took the major step of trusting God with a huge challenge that was facing me. I'm so glad I didn't miss those opportunities to hear God speaking to me as his Spirit moved through this place.'

During my lifetime, I have sat through many

church services and small-group meetings during which it seemed as though nothing special was happening inside me. But I have also sat through similar services and meetings during which my heart was turned inside out and my life was turned around. There was no way of knowing in advance when God would choose to use the meeting of Christians, the teaching of the Word, the lifting up of voices in worship or the sharing of personal testimonies to touch me in a unique and powerful way. Only an advance decision to come together with other Christians consistently could have put me in the right place at the right time to receive God's gifts of guidance and growth.

Even when I am on vacation, I try to join with local groups of believers. During a recent summer study break, I attended a small African-American church in Michigan. One Sunday the pastor gave a sermon about pursuing our calling from God with diligence; it was just what I needed that day. I shudder to think where my life would be had I decided to miss that church service, and so many others like it, which have provided me with the biblical teaching and the worship experiences I have needed to grow.

Before I move to one last component of discipline, I want to suggest an exercise that has been extremely helpful to me. Take a few minutes to reflect on the essential commitments that you believe God has called you to make. Consider issues like maintaining sexual purity, establishing healthy friendships, pursuing academic achievement, working with diligence, being a wise and loving parent, being a faithful spouse, caring for the poor, honouring your parents and using your spiritual gifts in the service of God and others. Then reflect on the critical decisions you need to make in broad daylight in order to fulfil these commitments. Think and pray and write about the ideas which come to your mind. Making a list of your commitments and putting your critical decisions in written form will help to confirm and strengthen them and will give you a visual reminder of the steps you need to take in order to get your life working the way you – and God – want it to.

Let's have a party

I call the fourth component of discipline *mini-celebrations*. If we intend to lead disciplined lives in the long term, we need to integrate little celebrations into the pattern of our lives. One of the dangers of becoming a highly disciplined person is that it is possible to plan and structure the joy out of life. I know; I've been there. And I ultimately reached a point of joylessness that forced me to learn a whole new way of understanding God's comprehensive plan for a disciplined life.

'A cheerful heart is good medicine,' says one proverb (17:22). Another says, 'The cheerful heart has a continual feast' (15:15). Cheerful was not how I would have described myself for many years. But that kind of lightness of spirit is what God wanted for me – and what he wants for you.

God knows how he built us and what will contribute to our well-being. He knows that we cannot lead chaotic, messy, unstructured, undisci-plined lives and still experience fulfilment. He knows that disorder and a lack of focus will eventually lead to anxiety, frustration and depression – and to lives that do not work well, lives destined to collapse destructively and tragically. So he invites us to well-ordered patterns of discipline that can put us on a path towards meaning and fruitfulness and fulfilment. He knows we need this.

But he also knows we need laughter and fellowship and fun and spontaneity and celebration; these provide a necessary, life-giving balance, so we don't inadvertently veer off the path of discipline and onto a deceptively similar detour that is legalistic, rigid, dull and draining.

When Jesus was on earth he modelled a well-ordered life that was liberally sprinkled with mountain walks, lakeside campfires, boat trips, wedding celebrations, leisurely dinner parties and overnight visits to close friends. He knew he needed to be disciplined about the important issues with which he had to deal, but he also knew he needed plenty of room for the kinds of activities and encounters that would contribute to this experience of freedom, pleasure, light-heartedness and joy. So he arranged his lifestyle so as to achieve that balance, and he invites us into a similar life of discipline and diligence, punctuated regularly with mini-celebrations that lift our spirits and make life sweet. I am seeking to emulate this kind of balance – and I love the effect it is having on my life.

So here we have it, this remarkable tool called discipline, with its four components of high goals, delayed gratification, advance decision-making and mini-celebrations. We can leave it rusting in the bottom of our tool boxes if we want to, but why do that? If we take it and put it to use, it has the power to transform the structure of our lives – and then there is no telling what we can do, what we can achieve and who we can become.

The choice is ours.

5
Speak truth

Surveys cited in business magazines and management books confirm that the personal characteristic employees most value in their employers is honesty; above all else, employees want to be dealt with truthfully. The same is true of employers. What they most want from their employees is the assurance that they can believe what their employees say and trust what they do.

When single people describe the perfect partner they dream of meeting and some day marrying, they inevitably say they want an honest man or woman who can be trusted in every way. They can't conceive of a marriage based on any other foundation than absolute trustworthiness.

Friends who have walked through life together for many years often name honesty as one of the keys to the success of their relationship. 'We made a commitment never to lie to one another,' they say.

In an age and a culture in which lies and deceit are common currency in films, books, chat shows, news reports and politics, the pursuit of honesty in personal life and relationships sometimes seems like a lonely and outdated endeavour. Yet these public displays of dishonesty have created in many of us an aversion to deceit that drives us towards the truth whether anyone else moves in that direction or not.

Of course, public displays of dishonesty are not the only sources of our repugnance. Most of us have been betrayed or lied to at least once or twice in such a brazen, hurtful way that we barely recovered. I mentioned in chapter one the time I described a secret, embarrassing part of my past to a Christian whom I thought was a friend. He encouraged me to speak openly to him by assuring me that he would never breathe a word of what I was saying to anyone else. As you may recall, two weeks later I almost lost my job because my boss had received some troubling information about me from my 'trustworthy' friend.

Because my boss was a wise and gracious man who was willing to listen to my accurate account of the truth, I ultimately did not lose my ministry. But the next time I saw the 'friend' who had betrayed me I was nearly blinded by my anger. I remember walking toward him in a public place, inwardly asking, 'Why? Why? Why did you do that to me?' My distaste for deceitfulness was firmly established that day.

Do you remember the first time you were betrayed or lied to? The first time a confidence was broken or the truth twisted in order to hurt you? I expect you remember that experience in vivid detail.

Did it make you want to withdraw from the human race? Did it make you want to stand up on a soapbox and shout at the top of your lungs, 'Would everybody please stop lying! Would everybody please start telling the truth!'

In case you're wondering, God wholeheartedly supports that idea. The Ten Commandments include a prohibition against 'giving a false witness against your neighbour'. In other words, 'Don't lie. Don't distort the truth. Don't use your words to misrepresent reality.' God knew from the beginning of time that without a radical commitment to telling the truth, marriages and families would disintegrate, friendships would explode, business dealings would fall apart, churches would be split by divisions, governments would become ineffective – the very fabric of relationships and society would unravel.

Throughout the Bible we are called to tell the truth, but nowhere more graphically and less diplomatically than in the book of Proverbs, where a man 'with a corrupt mouth' is called 'a scoundrel and villain' (6:12) and where the suggested response to lying is that 'a perverse tongue will be cut out' (10:31). Dishonesty is bad, says the writer of these proverbs, and we need to get rid of it – whatever it takes!

A path of destruction

One reason the author of these proverbs spoke so adamantly against 'a corrupt mouth' is that he knew how deeply dishonesty disrupts one's relationship with God. 'The LORD detests lying lips,' says Proverbs 12:22. Seldom does the Bible use stronger language than this to describe God's response to sinful behaviour. God *detests* lying. It's like saying it turns his stomach; it makes him sick. That's why he can't maintain fellowship with a person who lies.

I'm sure the reason God detests dishonesty so much is due to the second consequence, which is that it destroys other people. Proverbs 15:4 says, 'The tongue that brings healing is a tree of life, but a deceitful tongue crushes the spirit.' How could a God who delights in loving and encouraging tolerate any act that 'crushes the spirit'?

Every week at church I meet many people who have had their hearts broken by lies and deceit and twisted truths. 'She promised to be faithful,' sobs a devastated husband who has just learned that his wife wasn't. 'He said he would never come home drunk again,' cries a thirteen-year-old boy reeling yet again from the rages of his alcoholic father. 'I finished the job because the contractor assured me he'd pay, but he didn't. Now how can I pay my workers?' On and on it goes – spirits crushed by dishonesty and deceit.

Many people lament that life is not working well for them; the mechanism keeps jamming on broken dreams and faded hopes and thwarted plans. In many cases, if you trace their disappointment back far enough you discover a trail of dishonesty. It may have started with a slight departure from the point of absolute truthfulness, but all too often that first dishonest step leads to deeper forms of deceitfulness and from there to out-and-out lies. Along the way, the dishonest person begins to experience the inevitable breakdown of his or her relationships with

God and with others, whether in the home, at school, at work, in the neighbourhood or at church. It's easy to place the blame on other people or on forces beyond one's control when the real cause of trouble is one's own careless or malicious mishandling of truth.

Have you told any lies lately? Any 'harmless' little half-truths? 'We'll have lunch some time.' Tell me another. 'I'll pay you back soon.' A likely story. 'Can I have just one minute of your time?' One minute? Really?

Do you ever exaggerate the truth? Tell a story and add something to it? Describe a personal accomplishment in inflated terms? Do you ever minimize the truth? Confess to a sin less serious than the one you committed? Suggest that it 'wasn't really all that bad'? Do you ever twist the truth to make someone else look bad? Have you ever described another person's words or actions without explaining their context and thereby made that person appear stupid or cruel? Have you ever got yourself into a hole and then felt tempted to tell a fib to get yourself out of it? Have you ever yielded to that temptation?

Do you remember how you felt the last time you lied? Most of us feel a little queasiness in our stomachs or a little heat on the back of our necks. But the worst thing is that we don't know what to do with our eyes. We have only two choices: to look the person we're lying to straight in the eye or to look at the floor. It takes a brazen liar to look someone in the eye. Most of us don't like to think that we are in that category, but if we fix our eyes on the floor it's a sure sign that our words are dishonest.

Either way, you learn over time that lying is a messy business. It's always going to be a messy business because we're created in the image of a truth-telling God. At the core of the character of God is an essence of purity that renders him incapable of dishonesty; because of the piece of that purity that is at our own core, it will always feel unnatural and incongruous for us to lie. There will always be warning bells and whistles going off in our minds and that sick feeling in our stomachs. We weren't created to lie.

So the only reasonable choice for any of us is to stop lying. Now. Completely. If we have even the slightest tendency to distort the truth – and who among us doesn't? – we need to say, 'From this day forward I commit myself, with the help of God, to speak only the truth, always and in all circumstances, for the rest of my life.' Such a commitment will inevitably improve our relationship with God and with everyone else. But we must be willing to draw a line in the sand and say, 'Enough is enough. No more half-truths. No more exaggeration. No more verbal misrepresentation of reality. No more lies!'

Fifty-nine or fewer

For those of you ready and willing to make a firm commitment to honesty, the book of Proverbs offers some refreshingly practical hints for your journey from deceitfulness to telling the truth.

The first bit of counsel is as straightforward as a word of wisdom can be. You want to sin less with your words? Then talk less. You think I'm joking?

Read Proverbs 10:19: 'When words are many, sin is not absent, but he who holds his tongue is wise.' That's why I love the book of Proverbs. I wish I could meet the man who wrote that verse.

I can almost hear him outlining his strategy: Are we serious about telling the truth? Then let's talk in practical terms. Let's draw a graph. Look at it this way. If you have three hundred conversations per week and you lie five times, your Lying Ratio is three hundred to five. You want to reduce the number of lies? Then watch this. If you have only two hundred conversations next week, you'll bring your number of lies down to 3.3. Have sixty conversations the following week, you'll lie only once. And here's the real beauty of the system. If you want to stop lying altogether, have fifty-nine conversations or fewer.

You laugh over this imaginary scenario, but I have found in my own life that the less I talk in a seven-day period the cleaner my conscience ends up being with regard to telling the truth. The less I talk, the less I exaggerate. The less I talk, the less I say things I regret. The less I talk, the fewer promises I make that I can't keep. I suspect the same is true for you.

With regard to talking less, Proverbs 15:28 offers some further counsel: 'The heart of the righteous weighs its answers, but the mouth of the wicked gushes evil.' At the end of the week, who will have made more progress toward becoming a person who tells the truth? The one who carefully monitors her words or the gushing person who lets whatever forms in his mind spew forth from his mouth? The

Bible would vote for the person who slows down, considers carefully and holds back.

The wisdom of Proverbs tells us that we don't have to participate in every conversation. We don't have to express every thought that comes to mind. We do have to pause and carefully consider our words before we speak. Computers, I'm told, have a spell-check function. (Having no personal knowledge of anything related to computers, I can rely only on what I'm told.) Proverbs suggests that we ought to have a lie-check function, a little switch that is flipped on just before we open our mouths. When ideas and words are forming in our brains, the lie-check mechanism would ask us two questions. First, are the words we are about to say necessary? If they're not, why say them? Why needlessly increase the volume of our words and thereby create more opportunities for sin? Secondly, are the words we are about to say true? Are they absolutely, unquestionably true? If they're not, we should not spend one more minute thinking them, let alone speaking them. How many deceitful and destructive words might be silenced if we took the time to consider those two simple questions?

Trading truth for tranquillity

But there's another side to telling the truth. Yes, we are called to avoid unnecessary words, to truth-test ruthlessly every potential word and to silence our words if necessary in order to keep from whispering any hint of a lie. At the same time, however, when a given situation demands that a word of truth be spoken, we are commanded to speak it without hesitating, without holding back and without considering the cost to ourselves, even if it costs us dearly.

This needs to be a growth point in my own efforts to tell the truth. By God's grace, at this point in my life I have little temptation to fabricate wild webs of deception or to create sinister distortions of the truth; as I consciously monitor my words for honesty, I sense God's affirmation of my growth in this area. But when it comes to saying the hard truths that certain people desperately need to hear, I too often find myself hesitating.

I have a friend who is slowly destroying himself with alcohol. It's a medical fact: his mind and body are slowly caving in because of his years of alcohol abuse. This deeply grieves me, yet in the history of our seven-year friendship, I have only once, three years ago, summoned the courage to tell him the truth about his addiction. Every month his condition gets worse. Soon his life will be hanging in the balance. Why do I stay silent? Why do I hold back the truth?

I have another friend whose approach to parenting is slowly destroying his oldest child. The father demands a high level of control, and he is determined to turn his sixteen-year-old son into a star athlete. But the boy isn't interested in athletics; anyone (except his father, apparently) can see his passion and talent for writing and performing music. Predictably, the father–son relationship is deteriorating month by month. The father keeps making new demands for athletic achievement; the son keeps drifting deeper into isolation. Why haven't I told the truth to that father? Why haven't I carefully described what I discern about the gifts and interests of his son and about the destructive patterns of control I see in the family? I've proved my love and respect for my friend in many ways during the years of our friendship; he knows I have his and his family's best interests at heart. Yet I am afraid to speak the truth. What is wrong with me?

If those two illustrations aren't painful enough for me to admit, here's another one. Recently I became acquainted with a man who is genuinely one of the kindest, most fair-minded men I have ever met. We've had numerous conversations about everything under the sun, and I have thoroughly enjoyed every one. But to date I have not had the courage to tell him about the most important truth in life – that God loves him and has opened heaven's doors to him because of Christ's death on his behalf. He told me that he has never attended a church and has no spiritual background, yet I have not shared with him even the most basic truths of the gospel of grace. What's the matter with me?

You know what's the matter with me. It's probably the same thing that is the matter with most of us. I shrink back from telling the truth because it might cost me something. It might create discomfort in the relationship. I might be misunderstood or rejected. God forbid that my alcoholic friend would tell me that his drinking habits are none of my business, that the father of the budding musician would tell me to stay out of his family life or that my new friend would stereotype me as a religious zealot. Wouldn't that be the end of the world?

The ugly truth about me is that too often I choose

111

peacekeeping over truth-telling. I silence words of truth because they might create ripples on the pond of my life, and I, like many people, demand tranquillity. I want smooth waters, not rough seas. That's the truth about me, and I hate it.

I need to be reminded of Proverbs 3:3: 'Do not let kindness and truth leave you; bind them around your neck, write them on the tablet of your heart' (NASB). What is the writer saying? That we must doggedly cling to the truth whatever happens, and not only cling to it but also reveal it to others who need to know it. *Do you find it hard to do this*? he asks. Then write the truth on the tablet of your heart so you can't miss it, and hang a necklace of truth around your neck so no one else can miss it either. Cling to the truth and reveal the truth – in your marriage and family, in your friendships, in your relationships at college or in the workplace and in the church.

This text is one writer's creative attempt to help us break the habit of being silent when we ought to speak. I suspect that his motive for doing so was that he knew what a difference telling the truth makes. He knew the power of truthful words to redirect the course of a human life; conversely, he knew what a tragedy it is when opportunities for transformation are lost because truthful words are withheld.

How thankful I am that over the years some godly people have dared to speak the truth to me. Time and again their words have altered the course of my life. When I was a child I went to a Christian camp where some courageous leaders discerned that although I was religious, I didn't have a clue what it meant to have a personal relationship with God. They asked me if I really knew what it meant to be a Christian. 'Have you ever asked Jesus Christ, the Saviour of the world, to be your own Saviour? Have you ever applied what he did on the cross to your own sins? Have you ever asked the lord of the universe to be the lord of your life? Have you ever taken this step? Are you ready to do so now?' Those young people risked embarrassment and rejection by probing into the life of a fairly cocky, self-assured little boy, but as a result of their questions I became a Christian. Where would I be spiritually if those camp leaders had been more devoted to peacekeeping than to truth-telling?

Later in my life an older Christian man had the courage to ask me what I was going to do with my life that would last forever. He took me for a ride in his car one night and said, 'Bill, I see you're very committed to your family business. I see you have lots of enthusiasm for making money and buying things and creating an exciting lifestyle. But what about spiritual things? What about God's plan for transforming people and changing the world? You're willing to put your best efforts into pursuing your agenda. But what about God's agenda?'

It was hard for him to say that because he knew I was immersed in a lifestyle that offered me everything I thought I wanted; why should I listen to him? But his words brought me face to face with the most fundamental questions a person can ask: What am I going to do with my one and only life? What am I going to do that will affect people? What am I going to do that will make a difference in the eternal scheme of things? Those questions haunted me and ultimately opened my eyes to God's calling.

Years later a close friend of mine said to me, 'I think it's time for you to get some Christian counselling. I know you pray a lot. I know you read the Bible and apply it to your life. But it seems to me that there is brokenness inside you that you probably won't be able to sort out without the help of a wise, caring, Christian counsellor.'

I did not like hearing those words. In fact, I wanted to knock the man's head off. I wanted to scream in his face, 'Mind your own business! I don't need a counsellor.' Of course, my response to his loving suggestion was a huge indication of my need for such help, but I didn't see that at the time. What I saw was that I was a picture of health in every way, and he had no business implying otherwise.

Several years after the fact, I am so thankful that this man was willing to pay the price for telling me the truth. I desperately needed to hear it.

Do not let kindness and truth leave you, says the book of Proverbs. Cling to the truth and reveal the truth. You have no idea how God might choose to use your words to transform a human life.

The right approach
But there is more in this text than a command to cling to and to reveal the truth. Notice that truth is linked to kindness. The writer is making the point that when we write on those tablets of our hearts and when we hang those necklaces around our necks, we must make sure there are two words written down, not just one. Truth and kindness go together.

To be like Christ, as Ephesians 4:15 tells us, we need to learn the art of 'speaking the truth in love'. Truth and kindness.

Truth and love. Other biblical passages speak of truth and grace. This combination of truth mixed with kindness, love and grace gives our words transforming power. One without the other can be deadly.

Those who go around speaking the truth without love brutalize others. They force truth into people's lives insensitively and they leave a trail of bodies in its wake.

Then there are those who overflow with kindness, love and grace to everyone they meet, but they never add to their tender words any difficult truths. So they leave a trail of sentimentality devoid of substance and strength.

This text offers the antidote to both brutality and sentimentality. Be unreservedly devoted to telling the truth, it says, but always tell that truth in a spirit of kindness, love and grace.

A couple of years ago a staff member came into my office and said, 'Bill, we've known each other for a long time, and you know I love you. For the most part, I'm really proud of how you are growing and who you are becoming. But there's one aspect of your life that I'm concerned about. Can we talk about it? Can I make some comments? If you agree to that, I promise that I will pray with you about this. We'll talk about it again if you want to. I'll help you in your personal growth in any way that you want me to. I'll commit myself to do whatever I have to for us to grow closer together as you deal with this. You know I respect and love you. Can we talk about this?'

What fault can be found with an approach like that? What am I going to do, throw him out of my office? The man says, 'I love you. I care about your life. I value our friendship, and I want to preserve it. I'll stick with you through thick and thin and help you in any way I can.' Why wouldn't I be willing to hear the truth after hearing words like those? The key, of course, is that I knew he did love me and care about my life. He had been a faithful friend to me for years. So I said, 'Fire away. Tell it like it is.' I'll never forget the conversation we had that day. What he told me proved to be crucial in my growth as a pastor and a leader.

Imagine another graph in bright colours. On the far left is a blue area with the word *truth* printed above it. On the far right is a yellow area with the word *love* written above it. In the middle is a green area where truth and love mingle. Where would you place yourself on that graph?

Are you the kind of person who prefers to live in the yellow area? Are you proud of your reputation for always offering a word of encouragement and freely spreading love and grace around? But do you shrink back from speaking words of truth? Do you pursue peacekeeping at the expense of truth-telling?

Or are you an outspoken person who pride yourself on living in the blue area? Are you fearless when it comes to confronting people with the truth? Do you enjoy 'setting people right'? But do you generally ignore that bit about kindness, love and grace? Do you tend to brutalize others?

116

The challenge is to move toward the green area and develop the supernatural ability to communicate truth with such a kind spirit that your words become a channel for God's transforming power.

I have learned over the years not to get too close to people who operate outside the green area. My heart can't take the blows of those who wield the knives of truth without love. However, it does me no good when someone gushes grace and love in a blind acceptance of me. It feels good for a while, but it doesn't offer me the challenge I need in order to grow. People who live in the green area, though – what a gift they are! I can give them access to my life, knowing I can trust their truthful words to pierce my immaturity, my lack of understanding or my self-deception but not mortally to wound my heart.

Will you forgive me?

I want to close this chapter with some advice that doesn't come from the book of Proverbs but that is essential for anyone who is sincerely committed to leaving all kinds of dishonesty behind. The advice comes from James 5:16, which tells us to 'confess our sins to each other'.

One of the best disciplines to which I have ever committed myself is the discipline of confessing any hint of dishonesty directly to the person most affected by it as soon as I am aware of it and then humbly asking forgiveness. Sometimes I am so blinded by my sin that I don't see it right away, but as soon as I see it I go to the person I have wronged. After asking for forgiveness I tell the person that I am dedicated to becoming someone who tells the truth, and I thank him or her for accepting my apology. If I respond to my sin of dishonesty any less seriously, I end up forfeiting all sense of inner peace and joy. Without sincere confession of sin I cannot get on with life and make it work.

Do you want to improve your truth-telling performance? Then accept the discipline of confession. Decide today that every time you distort the truth or fail to live by your words, you will confess it to the person you have wronged. And don't assume that it is enough to confess only the out-and-out lies and the intentional deceptions. What about when you say you'll turn up and then you don't? Or you promise to be on time and then you arrive late? Or you agree to ring someone and then you never get around to it? Is that an honest way to live? Does it allow people to build confidence in what you say?

Imagine how our families, colleges, neighbourhoods, workplaces and churches would change if everyone were committed to speaking only the truth in love. It can happen, but it has to start with you and me. We can't control anyone else's choice of whether to speak the truth or tell lies. But we can make that choice for ourselves. We can take the steps we need to take to become loving truth-tellers.

Perhaps some of you who are reading this book should put it down now and open your hearts to God. Perhaps you need to make a commitment to speaking less so you can give more careful thought to your words and make sure that each one is necessary and true. Others among you may need to commit yourselves to learning that delicate balance between truth and love; you need firmly to establish yourself in the green section of the graph so you can avoid the extremes of both brutality and sentimentality. Others among you may need to take a step you've never taken in any area of your life, which is to commit yourself to the daily discipline of confession.

If you sense the Holy Spirit's prompting regarding confession, you could begin now by confessing your sins of dishonesty to God. If you do, I believe you will sense from God a response something like this: 'I know all about your lies, your exaggerations, your half-truths, your broken promises, your careless commitments. I listened and watched as your turned your back on me and yielded to every one of those temptations. But I love you anyway. No matter how far you have strayed, no matter how deeply you have allowed deceit to enter into your life, I still love you. If you're willing to turn from your sin, open your heart to me and trust in what Jesus my Son did for you on the cross, I'll forgive your sin, release you from guilt and gradually transform your life.'

If, as you pray, you hear a voice inside that berates you, criticizes you and makes you feel worthless, that voice is not God. If you hear a voice that sweetly says how good you are and only brings to mind all the great things you've said and done, that is probably not God either. But if you hear a voice that expresses unconditional love, accepting you completely with all your strengths and weaknesses, being absolutely honest about your gifts but also about where you need to change, that is very prob-

119

ably God speaking to you. He is, you see, the One who offers us the priceless gift of truth and grace because he is the One who matchlessly combines these in his being. So we can listen to him with joy because he is honest, and we can listen to him with joy because he loves us as no other does.

6
Choose friends wisely

For many years Lynne, Shauna, Todd and I have spent our summer holidays at our lakeside cottage in a little tourist centre in Michigan. Often in the early evenings we sit on a grassy bank above the Lake Michigan beach and watch people walk along the water's edge. Walking on the beach is one of the major pastimes in that quiet town. Sometimes we see solitary walkers, but more often than not we watch people walking in pairs or in little clusters. Some walk silently, but most seem to be engaged in pleasant conversations. The same is true of the people I see strolling through city parks when I travel or the ones I see walking through my neighbourhood when I'm driving home from work. Walking and talking seem to go together quite naturally.

Many times I too have enjoyed the pleasure of walking and talking with family members and close friends, and I have learned that during these walks neither the value of the walking as exercise nor the destination of the walk is important. What is important is having the opportunity to share thoughts and feelings in a relaxed, unhurried manner with someone with whom we want to spend time.

More often than not, when people say, 'Let's go for a walk,' they're using code language for an invitation into a deeper relationship. It is another way of saying, 'I'd like to open up my heart to you and have you open up your heart to me.' Many people, myself included, carry fond memories of walks that proved to be significant in the development of a relationship. In some cases, a conflict was resolved; in others, a commitment was made or a bond established. Such walks are never forgotten.

The book of Proverbs talks about walks like these, but not the kind that last a few minutes or even a few hours. When Proverbs speaks of walking with friends, it refers to the kind of walks we enjoy with a handful of companions over the course of many years, sometimes even a lifetime.

Most of us have casual friends, acquaintances and colleagues at work who pass in and out of our lives. But if we are fortunate, we will also develop a few close friends who become increasingly important to us as the years go by. Beyond our families, these people are the VIPs in our personal lives. We socialize with them, join in activities with them, enjoy deep fellowship with them and sometimes even go on holiday with them. In significant ways, our lives become intertwined.

The Bible frequently extols such friendships. One

particularly rich passage is Ecclesiastes 4:9–12, which says, 'Two are better than one, because they have a good return for their work: If one falls down, his friend can help him up. But pity the man who falls and has no one to help him up! Also, if two lie down together, they will keep warm. But how can one keep warm alone? Though one may be overpowered, two can defend themselves. A cord of three strands is not quickly broken.'

This passage and many others suggest that we all ought to build little teams of people with whom we can walk through life – people who help us try again when we fail, encourage us when we're discouraged, lighten our workload when it gets too heavy to bear alone, comfort us (as this passage says, 'keep us warm') and give us strength against the evil forces, temptations and trials we all face.

But the book of Proverbs offers some words of warning about walking through life with friends. Proverbs 13:20 says, 'He who walks with the wise grows wise, but a companion of fools suffers harm.' Yes, we all ought to walk closely with a few friends. But we need to be very careful, says the writer of this proverb, about whom we choose as friends. Wise friends will make us wise; foolish friends will bring us harm.

According to this proverb, close friends are more deeply connected than we might think. Though we may view ourselves as independent individuals, we are joined to our close friends by something like permeable membranes, those ultra-thin walls through which tiny particles can pass back and forth. What passes between close friends are values, convictions, morals, habits and goals. They pass back and forth whether we realize it or not, so despite our illusions of individuality, we end up being deeply affected by either the wisdom or the foolishness of our friends.

This means that we can increase our chances of growing in a positive way by choosing the right people with whom to become friends. If we want to develop sober judgment, we should choose friends renowned for making wise decisions. If we want to strengthen our convictions, we should pick people with reputations for standing up for what they believe. If we wish we were kinder, we should spend more time with those who treat others with gentleness and grace. If we want to walk more closely with God, we should put ourselves under the influence of people who make spiritual disciplines a priority. Choosing the right friends is like putting together our own personal development team; it will greatly improve our efforts in moving forward on the right path.

But the converse is also true. Foolish friends can ruin us. Their folly can seep into our lives and taint our desires and goals. Their faulty moral compasses can steer us off course. Their distortions of the truth can undermine our understanding of God and his ways. 'Do not be misled,' says 1 Corinthians 15:33, 'bad company corrupts good character.' If we let ourselves be corrupted, we'll pay; as Proverbs says, we'll 'suffer harm'. I know this is true; I've heard a thousand variations on this theme. It is uncanny how often people whose lives aren't working well can trace their downfall back to the choice they made to forge a friendship with a foolish person and who corrupted them in some way.

As I listen to these people tell their stories, I try to convince myself that I am different from them, an exception to the rule. I try to tell myself that I have walked with God long enough and have become stable enough and can hear the whisper of the Holy Spirit clearly enough that I could spend any amount of time with any kind of person and remain unaffected. I would like to think that. But when Paul wrote to the Corinthians, 'Do not be misled,' he was also writing to me. If I think I am an exception to this rule, I have been deceived. I, like anyone else, will become like the people to whom I choose to be close.

What kind of person do I want to become? And what about you? Once we clarify that issue, the rest is rather academic. We choose to walk with people whose thoughts, words and actions are such that we would like to claim them as our own. I am not talking here about personality, lifestyle, spiritual giftedness, talents or career; our close friends may be very different from us in these areas. What I am talking about are the deeper issues of integrity and character. If we are committed to following God's path and growing in the areas discussed in this book – wisdom, initiative, goodness, discipline, truth, and so on – then we should take steps to surround ourselves with people who exhibit those qualities. As our friendships with those people grow, so will our character and our pursuit of godliness.

Don't get too close!

The book of Proverbs offers practical advice about how to put together a team of walking companions who can help us move forward on God's path. The first advice I'd like to highlight is negative; it tells us what kinds of people should not be candidates for our team. It tells us that if we see certain characteristics in people, we should definitely cross those people off our list of potential close friends.

That does not mean they don't matter to God. They do matter to God, and we should use every opportunity we have to affect their lives in a positive way; we should be kind to them, serve them, love them and patiently point them toward the love of God and the gospel of grace, forgiveness and reconciliation. But they are not the people we should invite to walk closely with us through life.

Who are these people? They are men or women who exhibit the traits described in Proverbs 6:16–19. According to this passage, 'There are six things the LORD hates, seven that are detestable to him: haughty eyes, a lying tongue, hands that shed innocent blood, a heart that devises wicked schemes, feet that are quick to rush into evil, a false witness who pours out lies and a man who stirs up dissension among brothers.'

Whenever we see any of these characteristics in a person, we ought to hear warning bells ringing. This is not the kind of person we should count among our intimate circle of friends. Again, this does not mean we should deem such a person insignificant to us or to God; it does mean, however, that we should never give him or her a position of influence in our lives.

Let's look at these traits a little more closely. First, this text tells us to avoid a close relationship with anyone with haughty eyes. This refers to someone with an attitude of superiority, someone who says, even if only with his or her eyes, 'I have value; you are worthless. I am a winner; you are a loser. I am a professional; you are an unskilled worker. I am educated; you are a drop-out. I am beautiful; you are plain. I am married; you are single. I am conservative; you are liberal. I am a career woman; you are a stay-at-home mother. I am spiritually mature; you are not.' (Any of these pairs could be reversed; haughty eyes can look both ways.)

Such arrogance is frequently denounced in Scripture, and one who exhibits it receives a dire prediction for the future. 'Pride goes before destruction,' says Proverbs 16:18, and 'a haughty spirit before a fall.' Do you want companions who are heading for destruction? Walking partners who are destined to fall? Then steer clear of people with haughty eyes. Do not let their view of life colour your view, and do not let their future become yours.

The second person to avoid is the kind of person described in the previous chapter: a man or woman with a lying tongue. We cannot walk closely with someone who is not consistently truthful without getting our hearts broken. Sooner or later we will pay the price for choosing such friends by being deceived or betrayed by them. It is inevitable, and the pain will be excruciating.

What is even worse, however, is that if we walk with people who treat the truth lightly we run the

127

risk of doing so ourselves. The leader of one of our young people's small groups recently told me of a family torn apart by the lies of a teenage son.

When he was fifteen, this young man became involved with a group of pupils who told 'little lies' to their parents, covering up where they were going, who they were going with and what they were doing. At first he felt uncomfortable; he had never lied to his parents before. But eventually he began to see this practice in a new light, as a harmless distortion of reality in which normal teenagers always engage.

Once he become careless about the truth, the slide into deeper deception was easy. Eventually he broke faith with everyone – parents, girlfriend, teachers. Not only did his blanket of lies hide a lifestyle of drug abuse and petty theft that landed him in deep trouble with the law, but also it forced him into the long and agonizing process of rebuilding others' trust in him.

Steer clear!

The next kind of person to watch out for is one whose hands shed innocent blood. You are probably thinking, 'I'm all right with this one. I'd never invite an axe murderer to be on my personal development team. There's no problem here.' But the principle implied in this passage covers far more than the physical shedding of blood. Innocent people can be destroyed in a variety of ways. It happens every time those who are weak or powerless are assailed by those who are strong. And every time it happens, God hates it.

The writer of this proverb tells us to steer clear of people who abuse their power and throw their weight around. Steer clear of people who devalue others. Steer clear of people whose hearts are not moved by the suffering, hardship and needs they see around them. Steer clear of people who take advantage of other people's vulnerability. You can be sure that if you walk closely with people like these, one day you too will become a victim of their insensitivity and misused power. Even worse, their way of thinking, speaking and acting will probably begin to rub off on you. Do you want to become as cruel and heartless as they are?

In addition, we are advised to steer clear of hearts that devise wicked schemes and feet that run quickly to do evil. The writer tells us to keep an eagle eye out for anybody who can design, implement and then justify dishonest, illegal or evil plans. These are frightening people who could spell disaster for any team of walking partners.

A few years ago I met with a Christian leader who had felt led by God to devote his life to trying to shut down the producers and distributors of pornography. At the time I talked with him, he had been doing this for several years and had learned more than anyone would ever want to know about the pornography industry. After listening to him on this subject, I asked him what kind of man or woman could possibly build a career in pornography, particularly child pornography.

He said, 'You'd be amazed at what people can justify. In the pornography industry, film directors call what's going on in the beds "acting". The government turns the other way and calls it "art". Producers and distributors call it "free enterprise". Video stores call it "entertainment". The consumers who buy this rubbish call it "a good night of fun". But while all of this evil rationalization is going on, thousands of children's minds and bodies are being abused and destroyed.'

Any person who can justify participating in or perpetuating an evil system such as the pornography industry is someone with whom you don't want to walk closely. But let's look at a less extreme example. What about the man who develops a business plan that borders on the illegal? Even if he steps over the boundary every now and then, he doesn't care, as long as he doesn't get caught. Do you want to walk with a slippery character like this? Or what about the woman who finds a way to make her expense claim at work cover a good portion of her personal living expenses? Do you want a woman like that on your personal development team?

Dishonest schemers ought to be tormented with a guilty conscience to the point where they choose to change. If they don't, if they can live with their deceitful ways, we need to keep our distance from them.

A crucial choice

The next person to avoid is a false witness who utters lies. On the surface, this sounds the same as the second warning against a man or woman with a lying tongue. But this verse warns against a specific form of lying: a slandering tongue. If we meet people who are quick to pass on damaging information about a third party or are unable to keep sensitive information confidential, we need to walk in the other direction – fast. It is not safe to get close to such a person.

Perhaps being in a fairly public form of ministry has made me unusually sensitive to the issues of privacy and confidentiality, but for whatever reason, I find it impossible to speak freely if I discern that a person with whom I am has the tendency to speak carelessly, dishonestly or maliciously about someone else. Even in casual social situations, if I am around a loose-tongued person, I keep quiet. I withdraw from the conversation, reasoning to myself that whatever comes out of my mouth will probably get spread all round the neighbourhood, and I don't want any more of that.

As I said at the beginning of this chapter, half of walking is talking. One major reason for walking closely with others throughout life is to have people with whom we can bare our souls, people with whom we can share our secrets, reveal our dreams and confess our sins, our fears and our failures. But we can't do that without the full assurance that nothing we say is ever – under any circumstances – going to be inappropriately repeated.

The other side of this warning is like a finger pointing at our own hearts; it is the reminder that few sins are as easy to yield to as the sin of slander. We all have sinful tendencies and inner wounds – insecurities, fears, jealousies, selfishness – that can drive us to use careless or dishonest words to tear down other people or to ruin their reputations. The last thing we need is to spend time with people who have made a habit of yielding to these temptations.

How long before we too become bearers of false witness against others? So the writer tells us to steer clear of such people. That will keep us from getting hurt, and it will lessen the likelihood of our falling into the same sinful pattern of behaviour.

The last kind of person to keep off our personal development teams is one who spreads strife among brothers. Proverbs 16:28 says, 'A perverse man spreads strife' (NASB). Do you know of anyone who frequently stirs up conflict? Have you ever tried to have a relationship with someone who has a habit of nursing grudges, is always wanting a pound of flesh, demands huge apologies or has a chronically unforgiving spirit?

Proverbs says people like that are perverse; they are determined to do what is wrong. The Bible does not consider the spreading of strife to be an idiosyncrasy we ought to tolerate. Absolutely not. It is an out-and-out perversion of what it means to have integrity, to be honourable and to exhibit godliness.

Why is spreading strife perverse? Because any person who has been miraculously reconciled to God through the work of Jesus Christ on the cross has received the Holy Spirit, and in receiving the Holy Spirit, that person has also received the spirit of reconciliation. That means that whenever a problem arises in a relationship, the Spirit of God starts whispering to that person, 'Let's not get this out of proportion. Let's not draw blood and cause unnecessary damage. Let's resolve this as quickly as possible.' Anyone who claims to be a follower of Christ but enjoys spreading strife has wilfully chosen not to listen to the voice of reconciliation that speaks within him or her and has deliberately turned away from what is right. That person has perverted the gospel of reconciliation.

Such a person delights in dwelling on disputes and alienating friends and can have no lasting place among people who want to walk together through life. Walking companions must have full confidence that every member of the team is committed to resolving conflicts and establishing peace. Look at the words of Jesus in Matthew 5:9: 'Blessed are the peacemakers, for they will be called sons of God.' Which would you rather have on your team? One who spreads strife among friends or one who is a peacemaker? One whom the Bible calls perverse or one whom Jesus calls blessed? It's for us to choose.

Polar opposites

Let's sum up the discussion so far. The writer of Proverbs tells us not to invite people into our closest circle of friends if they have haughty eyes, a lying tongue, hands that oppress, hearts that devise evil plans or feet that carry them out. The passage also tells us to exclude from this group people who spread lies about others or who deliberately create strife. Building close relationships with such people is risky, and the stakes are so high that we can't afford to take the risk.

Now look back at our key verse, Proverbs 13:20: 'He who walks with the wise grows wise, but a companion of fools suffers harm.' According to Proverbs life's not going to work if we surround ourselves with the wrong kinds of people. We need to walk with wise and godly people.

Who are wise people? They are the opposite of fools. Who are godly people? They are the opposite of the people described in the last few pages of this book. They are people whose character contrasts with the seven traits that are 'detestable to God'.

Instead of a proud and arrogant person with haughty eyes and a spirit of superiority, we ought to look for a humble person with a teachable spirit, a person who delights in serving and encouraging others, a person whose intimacy with Christ draws him or her into a heartfelt union with everything and everybody Christ himself loves.

Instead of a person with lying lips we should look for a person with a record of speaking the truth. We should choose friends who by their example call us to a higher level of honesty, friends whose mere presence challenges us to think before we speak and to apply the standards of truthfulness discussed in the previous chapter. This is at the top of my list of what I look for in a friend. I need people around me who have committed themselves to honesty and who aren't afraid to challenge me to do the same.

Instead of people who are hard and cruel and insensitive, instead of people who use power and strength to destroy the weak and innocent, we must choose friends from among those who are tender-hearted and merciful. From the words of the prophets in the Old Testament to the words of Jesus in the New Testament, the Bible calls us to fight for the cause of freedom, to lift up the downtrodden, to bring healing to the sick, to care for the abandoned, to bring comfort to the grieving, to minister to the imprisoned, to offer food and shelter to the genuinely needy and to serve in a host of other ways. Imagine what the world would be like if you and I were more obedient to these biblical imperatives. Imagine the power for good that would be unleashed in a group of friends who spurred one another on to tangible acts of love and grace.

Instead of people who pursue and perpetuate plans that cross the boundaries of legality or morality, we must seek friends of great integrity who are beyond reproach, friends who will pull us toward higher levels of character, not lower. If we meet a person who is so purehearted that he or she troubles our conscience a little, we ought to consider pursuing a deeper friendship with that person. If we truly want to become more purehearted ourselves, that uncomfortable little pricking of our conscience may be just what we need. It may keep us walking straight down the path of integrity, where God wants us to be.

Instead of a loose-tongued person who will break our confidences and probably break our hearts, we need to look for people to whom we can bare our hearts and souls, knowing that the gold in the Bank of England is more vulnerable than the information we just shared. Such friends will provide for us a safe place in which we can authentically explore the depths of our spiritual lives, our feelings and our relationships. Being able to do this within the context of a loving, Christian community may allow us to reach levels of growth and healing that we could not reach in any other way.

Instead of a person who spreads strife, we need to seek friends with a reconciling, forgiving spirit who are committed to working through conflicts quickly. Disagreements are inevitable in any relationship, but if the people involved are willing to yield to the inner challenge of the Holy Spirit, conflicts can become avenues for personal growth and deeper bonding.

Does it sound good to be surrounded by a little band of people with humble souls and honest words and serving hands and pure hearts and listening ears and reconciling spirits? Would you like to walk through life with friends like that? Are you ready actively to pursue significant relationships with wise people?

In the banana room

Or does it sound like too much work or seem unrealistic? Are you afraid it is too late for you to put together a walking team? If so, read on. Everything I have written up to this point is common sense; it is a general review of what most people probably already know. But this chapter is about to take a turn – a turn into the banana room.

The banana room was a temperature-controlled and soundproof compartment in the warehouse of the produce company my family owned while I was growing up. When I worked at the company as a teenager, I knew that whenever my father took someone into the banana room it was because he wanted to have a strategic talk with that person. When I or other workers heard him call an employee into the banana room, we thought, *Oh my goodness. It must be serious*. We knew that going to the banana room with Harold was never something to take lightly.

Well, it's time for a banana-room conversation. A serious challenge from me to you.

I have been in the ministry for more than twenty years. During these years I have seen literally thousands of spiritually minded, intelligent, well-meaning people search with a vengeance until they found the right doctor, the right dentist, the right accountant, the right lawyer, even the right tennis coach. But when it came to searching for the right friends to walk with for the rest of their lives, there was no diligence, no careful searching, no aggressive pursuit. In regard to friendship, these otherwise thoughtful and energetic people seemed to be passive, uninterested and unmotivated.

This has never made sense to me, and I hope it never does. Beyond our immediate families, our close friends are one of the most significant keys to our personal growth and joy. They provide us with tremendous resources of insight, wisdom and counsel. They multiply our pleasures and mitigate our pain. They enrich the quality of our lives far more deeply than any goal we can achieve, any possession we can acquire and any position we can attain.

In my humble opinion, life loses half its meaning when it is not shared with close friends. What good is a birthday or an anniversary or a graduation without close friends to celebrate it? What good is a promotion without close friends to rejoice in it? What good is a dining room, a college room, a back garden, a patio, a guest room, a cottage or a boat without friends to fill it? We were born to experience life in a small community of close friends. They add the colour to the black-and-white events of daily life.

Friends also support us when tragedy strikes us or our families. They are the ones we can cling to when the phone rings and the words on the other end of the line make our blood run cold. Much as I hate to think about it, I know those calls are coming, and I don't want to be alone when they do. What about you? Proverbs 17:17 says, 'A friend loves at all times, and a brother is born for adversity.' Consistent love and help during rough times are two of the invaluable gifts that close friends – brothers and sisters – offer us. Why shouldn't we pursue them?

Life and death

Almost twenty years ago I became deeply convinced of the need to put together a personal life-development team. A man I respected challenged me deliberately to select a few men with whom I could walk closely in the next stage of my life. I was naive enough to think, *Maybe there is value in doing this. Maybe it will work.* I chose three men from my church; they were all older than I was, but we had much in common. Together we decided to try to work out what it meant for us to live in community.

We started meeting for lunch and then went on a few trips together. Slowly we began opening up our hearts and souls to each other – no small thing for three middle-aged businessmen and a pastor in his mid-twenties. Eventually we achieved a depth of relationship greater than any of us had ever experienced before. In time we felt the freedom to reveal our secrets, to confront one another about sins or mistakes or lapses in judgment, to cheer one another

138

on and generally to help each other grow up. It was amazing and wonderful. We described ourselves as a band of brothers.

Then, in the middle of that great adventure, one of the men learned that he had a brain tumour. I'll never forget those days when the three of us drove solemnly to his house. He had been a strong and brilliant man who had effectively run a business with several hundred employees. He had also been a loving husband and a devoted father and stepfather. But there he sat on his living room couch in a bathrobe, losing his hair, his colour, his strength – dying. For hours we sat with him. We told him jokes. We read the Bible to him. We prayed with him. We walked him to the bathroom. We helped him into bed when he was tired.

Night after night we drove away from his house with lumps in our throats so big we couldn't even talk to each other. Later, when he could no longer be cared for at home, we sat in his hospital room, quietly telling stories, reliving memories and praying.

Then came the phone call to say that the end was near. The three of us dropped everything and rushed to the hospital. We met in the lobby and headed for the elevator with dread in every step. By the time we got to his room, he had died; we stood by his bedside while the doctor pulled the white sheet over his head. Then we walked to a restaurant across from the hospital and sat in silent grief.

I remember speaking at his funeral service. The two other men served as pallbearers. I remember the graveside ceremony where, after I concluded my remarks, the casket was lowered into the ground. I remember the three of us walking back to our cars while in the distance the chimes in a bell tower pealed 'Amazing Grace'. I remember all this as though it was yesterday. The memories have so much texture; they're so vivid.

The pain of grief was not what we had anticipated when we entered into the covenant of friendship. But throughout that time, we knew that we were doing the best thing we could possibly have been doing. We were doing life – and death – together. We were living and loving and growing and changing and laughing and crying through adversity all the way to the end. Later, we would all look back on that time as one of the richest of our lives.

A necessary risk

This life that you and I are living today is real life. This is not the trailer for the film or television programme. This is it. This is the one and only chance we get at this great adventure called living. The Bible says the whole grand adventure was designed to be experienced in community. So one of the most critical decisions we face is the people with whom we choose to have this adventure.

I want these words to have an effect. I want passive people to start getting enthusiastic about friendship. It would be easy for you to say you have more important things to do, that identifying people to join you on this great adventure of life is not top of your list of priorities. Don't think that if you wait long enough three close friends will turn up on your doorstep, ring your doorbell and say, 'Here we are.

Let's live the rest of life together.' It doesn't work like that.

We each need to take initiative in this matter. We need to take risks. If we want to make life work, we need to put together a personal development team. If we want to become all God has in mind for us to be, we need to surround ourselves with godly people who can challenge and encourage us. If we want to experience the adventure of life fully, we need to put together a group of friends who can share its joys and sorrows with us. If we only have one chance at life, why not do it in the way God designed it to be done? Why not link arms with some brothers and sisters and walk closely with them?

Where to start? Begin mixing as frequently as possible with the kinds of people who might be potential members of your walking team. You probably know the places, activities and events that draw the kinds of people whose influence you would like to have in your life. You probably know where to find the people who are trying hard to know God better and to make a positive difference with their time, energy and gifts. Begin to spend your time where people like that live and work and play and go to church. Then be willing to make the first move. Introduce yourself. Shake hands. Begin conversations. Issue invitations.

One Sunday morning in the autumn of 1976 a man walked out of the Willow Creek Theatre, where I and a group of secondary school pupils and college students had started a church a year earlier. He walked past me and out of the huge glass doors overlooking the asphalt car park. Then he stopped, turned back, shook my hand and said, 'Would you like to play a game of rackets with me this week?' He ultimately became a member of the board of directors of my church and even more significantly, one of the founder members of the little band of brothers I just described to you. He and I are still close friends and will be until the day one of us dies.

What if he hadn't made that first move towards me? What great adventures might we have missed during the twenty-three years that we've been friends?

The adventures await. The only way to avoid reading a chapter like this in five years and being in the same position you're in now is to take some first steps. Perhaps one or two or three of the people you meet will become lifelong friends. It doesn't take long to discover how great it is to know that there are a few people in the world who know you, love you and are deeply committed to you.

7
Marry well

The first time I read the book of Proverbs, I was a little surprised by its straightforward manner in addressing the subject of marriage. After many years of study and analysis, I have concluded that the wisdom of Proverbs regarding the selection of a marriage partner can be condensed to four words: Don't mess it up.

I think the writer of Proverbs would tell us not to worry if we slice a golf stroke, lose a family heirloom, burn the Christmas turkey, dent a bumper on the car, do badly in a quiz or say something stupid to our boss. 'But,' he would say, 'don't make a mistake when you are choosing a marriage partner. Don't subject yourself to years of heartache and pain. Don't mess it up!'

In numerous passages the Bible makes it clear that God intends marriage to be a lifelong partnership. That is why the stakes are so high and why Proverbs uses such strong and colourful language to remind us of what it is like to be in an unhappy marriage. 'Better a meal of vegetables where there is love than a fattened calf with hatred' (15:17). Anyone in a struggling marriage knows how painful it is to sit in a beautiful restaurant staring down at a juicy steak for which you have lost your appetite. Who feels like eating when the person with whom you are sharing the meal seems more like a stranger than a lover and the distance between you seems more like a million miles than the width of a table?

Proverbs continues that theme in two famous verses. 'Better to live on a corner of the roof than share a house with a quarrelsome wife' – or husband (21:9). Living in a corner of the attic might be bad, but according to the writer of Proverbs, it is nothing compared with living with a contentious spouse – and sometimes even the attic is too close for comfort. 'Better to live in the middle of the desert than with a quarrelling, ill-tempered wife' (21:19). And obviously the same is true with an ill-tempered husband. The desert may be hot and miserable, but it is better than . . . well, you get the drift. The writer is saying that we would be better off anywhere than in a binding relationship with the wrong person.

How can this kind of tragedy and pain be avoided? How can people end up in a lifelong marriage that offers love, intimacy and happiness rather than loneliness, disillusionment and heart-break?

In *Finding the Love of Your Life*, Neil Clark Warren describes seven deadly errors that often contribute to badly matched marriages. Because I believe it is so worth pondering, I am going to include his list in this chapter.

Take it slowly

The first error young couples often make is to marry too quickly. Warren cites a Kansas State University study that establishes a strong correlation between long courtships and satisfying marriages and an equally strong correlation between short courtships and heartbreaking marriages.

For more than two decades I have been urging courting couples to move slowly toward marriage. Rarely do couples caught up in the excitement and passion of love want to hear about applying the test of time to their relationship. But they need to listen. They have everything to gain and almost nothing to lose by developing their relationship slowly over a long period of time. Every month of extended courtship either affirms or erodes their confidence in the health of their relationship.

Either way, it is a winning deal. If a couple discovers over time that the relationship is not all they thought it was, if they stumble upon irreconcilable differences or find that the spark is dying, they have been saved from a disastrous decision. Better to discover the truth about a relationship before marriage, when breaking up is an honourable option rather than a violation of marriage vows. If, however, partners discover along the way that their wildest dreams (or at least their earnest hopes) about love and intimacy are being fulfilled in their mutual, growing relationship, they can move toward marriage with greater peace and confidence and joy.

As ludicrous as it sounds to starry-eyed lovers, from the time their relationship becomes extremely serious, they should consider going out for a minimum of one more year. How can a couple go wrong by spending two, three, even four years moving from a casual relationship to a wedding ceremony? Are they afraid the feeling will go away?

That is the point – the feeling will go away, sooner or later. The high-intensity emotion associated with initial attraction and romance will settle into something else. The question is, What does it settle into? Boredom? Disillusionment? Frustration? Emptiness? Loneliness? Sadness? Or does it settle into a deeply satisfying and mutual friendship? Does it settle into a relationship that feels comfortable and yet challenging, safe and yet stimulating? Only time can answer those questions.

Another benefit of stretching out a courtship is that it allows parents and close friends time to observe the relationship. We would all like to think we are wise enough to make the major decisions of life alone, but we are not, especially when it comes to love. We need the insights and good judgment of those who have known us well for many years and have our best interests at heart.

There is so much that potential spouses need to learn about each other, and again, the stakes are incredibly high. To every couple I say what I have said for years, and what I say to my own children: Go slowly.

Grow up first

The second mistake that leads many people into unhappy marriages is that they go through the spouse selection process when they are too young. Why don't we let three-year-olds play with knives? Why don't we let eight-year-olds drive cars? Why don't we let twelve-year-olds make public policy? Because they haven't reached the stage in their development necessary for them to handle those responsibilities wisely. They may not be bad, stupid or immature. But they are children! And children should not be asked, expected or allowed to assume adult responsibilities.

Few responsibilities in life are more daunting than the responsibility of selecting a spouse. Yet many people take on that responsibility prematurely, before they have the combination of discernment, life experience and personal maturity required to make such a decision wisely.

Not only are they hindered in making a wise decision by their own youthfulness and immaturity, but what about the potential spouse? How do they know who that person is going to become in two years or three years or five years, when he or she has grown up a bit? Experts in psychological development now believe that few human beings reach a point of psychological maturity before age twenty-five.

Most people younger than that are engaged in the intense work of establishing identity. They are trying to answer one of the most crucial questions in life: Who am I, really? In terms of personality and preferences, people in their early twenties are still being formed.

Most people under the age of twenty-five are also deeply involved in the process of separating from their childhood home. They are asking complex questions: Who am I separate from my family? How do I gain autonomy from my parents and my siblings? What does it mean to lead my own life?

Most people under twenty-five are still in the midst of determining their core values. They are asking probing questions: What things are most important to me? What do I believe about life and relationships and work and the future? What do I want to establish as priorities? What are the non-negotiable values I want to live by?

Most people under twenty-five are also actively engaged in developing their skills. Through education, jobs and a variety of life experiences they are trying to answer questions like these: What am I good at? How can I best develop my gifts and abilities and talents? What kind of career should I pursue?

Finally, most people under twenty-five are engaged in the work of spiritual formation. Even if they have answered the following questions as children, they often ask them again, on a deeper level, as young adults: Do I really believe in God? Do I really believe that Jesus Christ is who he said he was? Do I really believe it strongly enough to arrange my whole life around pursuing God and following the teachings of Christ?

During this critical era of growth and change, how can anyone be expected to be making a decision as important and far-reaching as the selection of a marriage partner? One author said it is like shooting at a moving target from a spinning platform. It is nearly impossible.

Statistically, divorce rates are lowest for men and women who wait to marry until they are twenty-eight years of age or older. The highest divorce rates are among those who marry during their teenage years or early twenties. The chances for a satisfying marriage are best for those who grow up first and marry later. Imagine that.

In love with being in love

According to Warren, the third reason people often make poor decisions regarding marriage is that they are too eager to be married. They have fallen in love with the notion of marriage, seeing it as the answer to all life's problems. *Marriage will end my loneliness*, they think. *It will heal my brokenness. It will ensure my happiness.* Often people who have had disappointing childhoods think that marriage can make up for all the toil, troubles and shortcomings of their lives; marriage will guarantee them the bliss they missed in the past.

Usually nothing is further from the truth. Rarely does someone who is seeking a spouse to 'offer me the life I never had' end up with a satisfying marriage. Rarely does walking down an aisle transform a chronically unhappy person into a joyful, vigorous, positive one. Rarely does the union of two sinful and wounded human beings lessen the challenge of life.

More than likely, unless personal issues are dealt

with first, entering marriage will only add to the burdens one already carries.

This isn't about pleasing others

The fourth mistake some people make is to move prematurely into marriage in order to please or placate someone else, usually parents or friends. Subtle hints get dropped at family get-togethers. Less-than-subtle suggestions fly at friends' weddings. Point-blank questions stun two people who are going out: 'So when are you two going to tie the knot? Isn't it about time we heard wedding bells?'

When a young woman's college friend comes home from a date, ring finger elevated to eye level, the pressure is on. Now another person has jumped on the conveyor belt and is moving towards marriage. *What is the matter with me?* the young woman wonders. Obviously, she concludes, the time has come to embark on a serious quest for a marriage partner. How else can she prove to other people that she is marriage material?

Really know each other

Other people make a mistaken choice because they have not shared a wide enough range of life experiences with their potential partner. Some couples decide to get married despite the fact that they have never come through a tragedy together. They have never resolved a conflict with one another. They have never negotiated a serious compromise over an issue on which they feel deeply. They have never worked through financial challenges. They have never learned anything important about each other's work. They have never worshipped or prayed or joined in Christian service together. They have never got to know each other's friends. They have never spent significant time with each other's families.

Couples who centre their whole courtship around a series of carefully planned dates may have lots of fun, but they will probably not get to know each other deeply. Sharing a broad range of experiences and seeing how a potential spouse speaks, behaves, relates to others and reacts in many different situations are the only ways to get a realistic glimpse of what it might be like to share the future with that person.

Who would want a marriage like that?

Many partners make the mistake of deciding on marriage without making sure that they have realistic and compatible expectations regarding marriage. This is the one that caught my wife and me off guard in our early years of marriage.

I grew up in a family in which my father and mother had a high degree of autonomy. My father would often leave for a business trip to South Africa, Eastern Europe or South America for several weeks, forgetting to tell my mother that he was going. When he landed on the evening of the first day, he would call my mother and say, 'Jerry, I'm not going to be home for dinner. I'm in Cape Town.' My mother would say, 'Okay, Harold, thanks for calling.' That is the kind of home in which I grew up.

Lynne's parents were the exact opposite. They were extremely close to one another. Her father worked just a few blocks from the house and often came home for lunch. He spent nearly every night at home, unless he was out with his wife, and he never travelled, except for family holidays.

Had Lynne and I talked about this before we got married, we undoubtedly would have realized that this was a potential problem. But we never talked about it. I don't think we even gave it much thought. I think I looked at Lynne's family and thought, *Well, surely Lynne doesn't plan to model our marriage on her parents' marriage?* She looked at mine and thought the same thing. Bad assumptions to make. Of course, neither of us planned to model our marriage exactly on our parents' marriage. But the truth is, we each believed that our parents were doing it right, and we each hoped to fall into a pattern similar to the one with which we grew up.

Then one day I forgot to tell Lynne I was going on a trip. It doesn't matter, I thought. I called her that night from Los Angeles to tell her I wouldn't be home for dinner. It did matter, she thought. At that point, we began having serious discussions about marital expectations.

Believe me, it is much better to talk about things like that before marriage. Partners need to think about and talk about the marriage models they hope to emulate. It is helpful to analyse the marriages of mutual friends and acquaintances. Discuss what you like and don't like about their marriages. Discuss how they communicate, how they resolve conflicts, how they make decisions together, how much time they spend together, what they do with their leisure time, whether or not they have any leisure time. Talk about expectations regarding family holidays, pace of life, degree of involvement in friendships with others, business travel. If your partner says, 'I really like how the Taylors' marriage works,' find out why. What does he or she like? It is crucial for partners to understand and compare their expectations. When it comes to marriage, are you both placing the same order?

Determining roles within the marriage is also critical. Do you both plan to have careers? Will you both continue your careers even if you have children? How will that work out? What about household jobs and childcare? Who will carry the weight of those responsibilities? Who will be financially responsible for the family? How do you think important decisions should be made? Who has the final say? Do you want a hierarchical marriage based on a structure of authority? Is one of you going to be a boss in your marriage, someone with a final say? Or do you want an egalitarian marriage based on the model of mutual submission, in which you both submit yourselves to God and one another and then trust the Holy Spirit to guide and rule your marriage?

These are important questions. When couples make assumptions rather than mutual decisions regarding issues as important as these, they are almost certain to end up in confusion and conflict. It is far better to make these decisions in advance, before the pressure is on.

Know the broken places

Finally, many couples make the mistake of deciding to marry without addressing personality or behavioural problems related to hidden emotional difficulties.

When a person is looking for a boat, the first step a potential boat owner takes is to get a survey – a thorough, professionally prepared evaluation of the boat under consideration. The survey will reveal if the boat has ever sunk, hit a reef, lost its mast or suffered any other kind of damage. It will also give details about past engine trouble. The survey is invaluable for a potential buyer because it provides the boat's complete history.

When it comes to looking for an aeroplane, the crucial documents are the maintenance records. In addition to giving details of routine maintenance procedures, these records explain any structural damage the plane has sustained and any past problems with the engines or electronic equipment. Like a boat's survey, an aeroplane's maintenance record offers a potential buyer information upon which to make an educated decision.

Wise buyers want as much information as they can get. It is not that they will never buy a boat or a plane with a problematic history. It is that they want to make that decision with their eyes open; they want to know what they are dealing with. They want to know exactly what went wrong and what was done to correct the problem. What repairs were made? What steps were taken to make sure the problem won't be repeated?

Sometimes I think potential spouses should be required to carry around surveys or logbooks explaining their history. It is only fair for people to know the traumas that have affected the lives of their potential spouses and how these traumas have been dealt with. Partners deserve answers to questions like these: What happened to you? How did it hurt you? What have you done to find healing for those hurts?

Later in this chapter I will address this subject further, but let me say at this point that we are all wounded and damaged in various ways. These wounds and this damage don't necessarily make us unfit for marriage, but they do have implications for marriage. It is only wise, then, to consider these implications carefully before we marry.

Now what?

Do you want to avoid the pain of living with or being a quarrelling, irritable, contentious, angry spouse? Do you want to avoid having to creep up to the corner of the attic in order to have a moment's peace? Then don't decide to marry too quickly or when you are too young. Don't marry because you have fallen in love with the idea of marriage or because you want to prove to somebody else that you are marriage material. Don't decide to marry until you have shared a variety of life experiences with your potential spouse or before you have decided what kind of marriage you want. Don't marry without understanding the wounds that both you and your spouse bring to the marriage.

I know this is a long list of don'ts. But the list of

155

frustrations, heartaches and pains compiled by those who ignore those proven guidelines for courtship is even longer, and all too often the list grows year by year. So please, if you are in the spouse-selection process, read back through the last few pages, write out Warren's list of deadly errors, reflect on them and then do whatever you have to do in order to avoid them. Don't think you are an exception who can ignore these cautions and warnings.

But what about the positive side of the spouse-selection process? What do we do once we have committed ourselves to all the don'ts? What do we look for in a potential spouse?

Contrary to what most of us believe, researchers in the area of marital success have concluded that what is most likely to make relationships work in the long term is similarity. That's right – numerous basic similarities. How many times have you heard it said that opposites attract? It may be true that they attract, but research shows that often the very things that initially attract two people later push them apart. That is not to say that personality differences between spouses are necessarily bad (more on that in the next chapter). But marriages based on differences, on the attraction of opposites, without an underlying foundation of core similarities are usually heading for trouble.

With this in mind, let me offer you five profoundly important areas of compatibility that should be in place before partners decide to stand together at the altar.

The God factor

The first and most important area in which spouses need to be compatible is their relationship with God. 'The fear of the LORD leads to life,' says the writer of Proverbs, 'and he who has it rests satisfied' (19:23 RSV). If knowing God 'leads to life', it would seem to follow that it is one of the keys to building a satisfying marriage and also something spouses should share in common. The Bible affirms that very thing. In fact, it offers strong teaching on this subject.

The apostle Paul wrote to the Christians in Corinth, 'Do not be yoked together with unbelievers' (2 Corinthians 6:14). His words can be applied to relationships other than marriage, but in no other relationship are we so intimately 'yoked together', so this verse is particularly pertinent to marriage. What it means is that a person who loves God and follows Christ should never marry a person who doesn't share those faith commitments. Why marry someone with whom you do not hold in common that which 'leads to life'?

Many Christian single people fume when they hear that as for obvious reasons it reduces the number of possible marriage candidates. To many Christian single people, this feels restrictive, almost punitive. They think, 'Was God having a bad day when he gave this command? I happen to be in love with a person who is not a Christian. What's so bad about that? Why can't I marry him (her)?'

But when thoughtful people reflect on this instruction from God, they begin to understand that it flows out of the idea of basic similarity. Again, research confirms that marriages between very compatible people tend to be more satisfying than marriages between people with less in common. What is deeper than a person's spirituality? What affects a person's basic identity more than the realization that he or she is a child of God? What transforms a person's heart more than the experience of being loved by God? What fills a person's life with more meaning than the continuing challenge of relating to God in a personal way? If you are a Christian, do you really want to marry a person who cannot relate to what shapes your identity, transforms your heart and gives you meaning in life?

It is one thing if partners do not share a mutual love for line dancing, football or Chinese restaurants. If other dimensions of the relationship are satisfying a couple can probably handle those differences. But when one spouse places God at the centre of his or her heart and life and the other spouse doesn't, that produces deep disharmony. When one spouse desires above all else to walk with God, to please God, to serve God and to proclaim God's goodness, and the other spouse couldn't care less about the things of God, there is bound to be some deep loneliness in that marriage.

Not long ago, after I had just spoken at a leadership conference in Seattle, a young man greeted me with these straightforward words: 'Three years ago I hated you. These days, I like you and respect you a lot.' He continued, 'Let me tell you what happened. I'm a Christian, and for years the aim of my life has been to know God and to please him. But several years ago I fell head over heels in love with a woman who was not a Christian. I was concerned because she wasn't interested in God, but she was a wonderful woman, and I was quite determined to marry her.

'Then I read the book that you and your wife wrote called *Fit to Be Tied*. In it you have a whole chapter on the necessity of spiritual compatibility. I was so angry with you because your words were messing up my plans. But after I thought more about that chapter, I realized that because God is so central to who I am and what my life is about, it would be a disaster for me to marry someone who is not concerned about the things of God. So I broke up with "the love of my life". I ended the relationship. She and I were both heartbroken, and you were not my favourite person – or hers – for a long time.

'A year later, however, I met a delightful woman who is as committed to walking with God as I am. Just last month, we were married. Thank you for challenging me to wait for a woman with whom I could share the most important things in life. We walk into our church together, and we sit down and learn from God's Word. We hold each other's hand and lift our other hands up to God as we pour our hearts out in worship. We pray together when we share meals. We invite our friends to church. Life has become a wonderful adventure that we are enjoying together as a married couple. I cannot imagine what it would be like not to share all this with the person to whom I have committed myself for a lifetime.'

I have heard hundreds of variations of that story. I have also heard the opposite kind of story. 'Five years ago I heard you give a talk about spiritual compatibility,' a young woman said to me, 'but I thought I knew better. So I married a man who is not a Christian. Not being able to talk with him about my walk with God has become my greatest source of sadness in our marriage and causes me more distress than anything else.'

One woman told me, 'I come to church alone every single week. My husband wants nothing to do with God and is disturbed that I'm a part of this church. Every night before I put my children into bed I pray with them, and my husband walks past and mocks me.'

Imagine the discord in that home. She prays with her children, and her husband walks past and laughs. What will happen when those children get to junior and secondary school and the father is still walking past laughing? By then, the children will probably be laughing too.

In *Fit to Be Tied*, Lynne and I wrote about the importance of spouses finding in God and in the Bible a common treasure, a common blueprint for living, a common set of values and a common strength in times of trouble. These are vital things to have in common. Do you share them with the person with whom you are going out? If you are in a relationship which is moving towards marriage, please answer that question honestly. Violating the biblical wisdom about spiritual compatibility is probably the most risky move you could make in getting married. Please, don't even think about making it.

The character factor

'The integrity of the upright guides them,' says the writer of Proverbs, 'but the unfaithful are destroyed by their duplicity' (11:3). As we have seen, this is a theme repeated throughout the book of Proverbs. In passage after passage we are told that sound moral character (integrity) will guide people along straight paths that bring rewards to them and honour to God but deceitfulness in speech or conduct (duplicity) will lead people to ruin.

What this means for selecting a spouse is clear. How could any of us hope to build a satisfying marriage with a person who lacks integrity? Perhaps if two people are equally deceptive, they may find some sort of twisted happiness together, but anyone striving to live with integrity before God and other people must marry someone who shares that goal. This is called character compatibility.

Imagine a situation in which one partner is committed to honesty while the other has a tendency to fudge the truth a little. Or one partner always honours commitments while the other breaks them habitually. Or one partner uses money responsibly so it is possible to save, tithe and help the poor while the other throws money away carelessly. Or one partner works with diligence and discipline while the other is lazy. Or one partner chooses friends wisely while the other always ends up with the wrong kinds of people. Or one partner is committed to sexual fidelity while the other considers it an option. These are not minor differences of opinion. Character disharmony can eventually destroy a marriage.

Character compatibility is what determines the level of trust in a marriage. Without trust, there is no foundation upon which to build a marriage. So please don't compromise with character. If you are considering marriage, look closely at your partner. Do you have complete confidence in his or her integrity? Can you trust him or her in every way?

The emotional health factor

The third area of necessary compatibility has to do with emotional health. This does not mean that two people have the same kind of emotional make-up or that they are at the same stage on the road to emotional health. It does mean, however, that they have reached a level of mutual understanding of each other's emotional histories that allows them to be confident that their future together will not be imperilled by secrets, hurts and complications from the past.

Let me be painfully direct here. That special person you are thinking about marrying – the one whose hand you hold under the restaurant table and who looks so irresistible in candlelight – grew up in a fallible family with imperfect parents and sinful siblings. That person more than likely came up against a few deeply troubled and sin-stained friends, teachers and, perhaps, pastors. You can be sure that your heart-throb did not make it into your life without making some blows along the way. But what kind of blows? How much damage was done? Has healing taken place? These questions need to be answered during courtship.

I remember talking with a young man who was on

the verge of proposing to a bright, young, Christian girl with whom he was head over heels in love. He described her to me, and then I casually inquired about her family background. 'Oh,' he said, 'nothing to worry about there. Her dad has been married and divorced twice and her mother is an alcoholic, but she has never let that affect her. She's really strong. I'm sure it won't be a problem.'

'All right,' I said, 'I'm not suggesting that you shouldn't marry this girl. But maybe you should slow down a little bit and take a more careful look at her family background.'

He waved me away by saying, 'Look, I assure you, it's not a problem. I know this girl. I've gone out with her for four months, and I can tell she's come to terms with all this. I'm going to marry her, and I'm sure it's going to be all right.'

Can you imagine how that marriage is going to work out if the partners never deal seriously with what it meant to grow up in an alcoholic family with a double divorce? I think that couple are going to have a very tough time.

'A prudent man sees danger and takes refuge,' says Proverbs 22:3, 'but the simple keep going and suffer for it.' In the Bible 'the simple' means those who live without thinking. Proverbs is saying that a person who thinks wisely sees a danger and works out what to do to avoid it, but the person who doesn't think walks straight into it and pays the price.

That is what so many couples do. I have heard story after story about men and women who knew their partners had been deeply hurt in the past and who knew the potential dangers to their relationship, but they thought they could bypass the problems, that everything would work out well in the end. Now they are trapped in living nightmares because they didn't take the dangers seriously. And the dangers are serious. Deep wounds from the past may produce fear of intimacy or abandonment; buried anger and rage; chronic depression; debilitating insecurities; phobias, obsessions and compulsive behaviour; codependency; alcoholism and other addictions. I could go on and on. Emotional wounds can be healed, but only if they are acknowledged and taken seriously.

Partners need to talk for many hours and over a long period of time about the bumps and bruises of life that they have experienced. They need to be honest with each other about things like childhood sexual abuse, growing up in a broken family, the addictions of a parent, unusual difficulties at school, unpleasant relationships with siblings or any other circumstances or events that caused physical or emotional distress.

What complicates this is that most young people are not very aware of their own hurts. That is why I have become such a strong advocate of individual and pre-marital counselling. Having someone who is competent and trustworthy ask the right questions, probe deeply into our past and help us uncover unhealthy influences can lead us to insights that can alert us to potential problems. Questions such as the following might be helpful as starting points for further discussions:

- Who were the most important people in your life, and how did they treat you?

- What are your best memories?

- What are your worst memories?

- What did you enjoy most about your family life?

- What event or circumstance in your life hurt you more than anything else?

- What negative feelings did you struggle with as a child?

- What negative feelings do you struggle with today?

Most people who go through pre-marital counselling come out on the other side much better prepared to make their life and marriage work. A close friend of mine and Lynne's grew up in a family in which there was alcoholism, sexual abuse and divorce. When this young woman was twenty years old she realized that she was incapable of sustaining healthy romantic relationships, so she went for counselling. Six years later she married a wonderful man and is now building one of the most delightful and satisfying marriages I have ever seen. She faced her deep hurts honestly and chose to take the steps that would lead to healing. Her choice is paying off.

No matter how damaged we have been by the unpleasant realities of life, we can get the help we need to learn and grow and heal. For all of us, that process will continue throughout our lives, but the sooner we begin it, the better it will be, for ourselves and for our potential spouses.

The talk factor

The fourth area of compatibility regards communication. The idea of two people communicating on a deep level sounds simple, but it is not so easy to accomplish. Many marriages fail because 'we just couldn't talk to one another'. Before marriage, a young woman may be charmed by the strong, silent type with whom she is going out. And a young man may be thrilled to have found a partner who is mysterious. But silence and mystery often prove to be deadly in a marriage. Couples whose marriages are flourishing list among their reasons for success the fact that they 'talk about everything'.

And they don't mean the weather and the children. They mean that they have learned to engage each other in deep conversations. Proverbs 20:5 says, 'The purposes in the human mind are like deep water, but the intelligent will draw them out' (NRSV). People in mature relationships learn how lovingly and patiently to draw deeply personal thoughts and feelings out of one another. They ask questions, they listen, they ask more questions, they wait, they gently probe, they affirm, they encourage. They provide a safe environment for the deep revelations that lead to true intimacy in marriage. But this takes two people who are willing to talk and willing to listen. It won't happen if both partners want to talk but never want to listen. Nor will it happen if one partner consistently assumes the role of the talker and the other partner consistently plays the listener. An authentic dialogue requires the full involvement of two parties.

People in mature relationships also learn how to speak the truth in love, as we discussed in an earlier chapter, and how to resolve conflicts without drawing blood or undermining the security of the relationship. They learn how to discuss hopes and dreams without making each other feel foolish. They become each other's most enthusiastic fans.

What about you and your partner? Can you talk? Can you listen? Can you probe gently into each other's hearts and souls? Are you both at least willing to try?

The physical factor

The final area of compatibility I want to discuss concerns physical attraction. Though this subject was talked about by everyone else, I never heard it discussed by a pastor in the twenty years I went to the church in which I grew up. It was as if this – the physical factor, the chemistry, the passion – were something illegal, even sinful, something better left to the secular world. Yet one of the most powerful examples of a strong physical factor comes not from Shakespeare or Hollywood but from the Bible itself.

In the book of Genesis, we read about a man named Jacob who met a woman named Rachel. Jacob felt such a powerful attraction to Rachel that the first time he greeted her with a kiss he 'began to weep aloud' (Genesis 29:11). After that, his attraction prompted him to volunteer to work for her father for seven years in order to earn her hand in marriage. (I think I might direct my daughter's next boyfriend to that passage!)

Jacob lived on the family farm with Rachel and

her extended family so they could court one another during the seven years he was working for her father. The Bible says that the couple so loved being together that 'seven years . . . seemed like only a few days' (Genesis 29:20). That redefines 'smitten', doesn't it? There was maximum chemistry at work there.

But then there was a little twist in the story. At the end of seven years, Rachel's father decided that his older daughter, Leah, needed to be married off before his younger daughter, Rachel. So he tricked Jacob into marrying Leah. Since having more than one wife was not forbidden in those days, Jacob's father-in-law then said he could marry Rachel the next week, but he had to agree to work for his father-in-law for another seven years. And this Jacob gladly did.

The point is that God designed each one of us with the capacity to feel a strong attraction towards certain people. If potential marriage partners don't feel that strong mutual attraction, there is something wrong. Proverbs 5:18–19 says, 'May your fountain be blessed, and may you rejoice in the wife of your youth. A loving doe, a graceful deer – may her breasts satisfy you always, may you ever be captivated by her love.' Could there be a clearer verbal picture of the physical component of love?

Kathryn Johnson wrote a book called *Lucky in Love*. She interviewed a hundred married couples whose relationships had flourished over many years. She was surprised to learn how important the attraction factor was both in building and in sustaining marriages. She called it a major force in stabilizing and enriching a relationship over a period of many years.

Though this strong attraction makes sexual restraint difficult during courtship – and make no mistake about it, the Bible calls us to sexual restraint before marriage – it pays off later. Many married couples are convinced that the physical factor was a gift from God to help them through difficult times in their marriages.

This is no justification for marrying the first person who makes your heart beat fast. However, do not underestimate the importance of mutual physical attraction. It is a significant component in the overall picture of a healthy marriage.

As you consider the seven errors people make in choosing a spouse and the five areas of compatibility necessary for a good marriage, also consider one last proverb: 'Plans fail for lack of counsel, but with many advisers they succeed' (15:22). Do not make this important decision alone. Do not make it without the input of the wisest, most godly and mature people you know – parents, teachers, pastors, couples whose marriages you admire and who have been married for ten, twenty, thirty years. Get help from many such sources. Openly set out for them the issues covered in this chapter. Then tell them to say whatever they want, no matter how hard it might be to hear. And then listen and listen carefully.

God invented marriage. He designed it to be a great joy, but it can also be a great challenge. We need a Christian community supporting us from the beginning of this wonderful enterprise. Starting well is the best way to make sure we finish well.

8
Forge strong families: Part one

All my life I have been impressed by people who have the ability to speak succinctly and with insight in the face of complex challenges. Consider, for example, Winston Churchill's words as France fell to Hitler in 1940 and people awaited the Battle of Britain. While many thought it prudent to come to a negotiated peace with Germany, Churchill was convinced that Britain must stand firm.

He rallied a downcast people whose prospects were bleak and whose future was far from certain with the words, 'We shall fight in France, we shall fight on the seas and oceans, we shall fight with growing confidence and growing strength in the air, we shall defend our island, whatever the cost may be, we shall fight on the beaches, we shall fight on the landing grounds, we shall fight in the fields and in the streets, we shall fight in the hills; we shall never surrender.' And so fear turned to hope, and the Nazi threat was turned back, and the course of the war was changed.

Or consider one of the other great speeches of the twentieth century. In the summer of 1963 as racial tensions stirred in the United States, Martin Luther King Jr planned a massive March on Washington in August. What would a quarter of a million people hear? A rejection of all that America stood for? A call to violence and hatred? No, instead they heard, 'I have a dream,' a dream of America at its best, a dream of racial harmony, a dream of human dignity that gave the civil rights movement clear direction and that decades later still awakens us to action.

As we move into the twenty-first century we are facing one of the world's greatest challenges: building strong families. Few people would deny that prospects look bleak for all too many families; many people even consider the traditional concept of a strong nuclear family dead – and for good reason. Though guns and bombs are not the chosen weapons in the wars that rage in many homes, the casualty list is often devastating. A hatred nearly as deep as that which fuels racial tensions lies beneath the surface of a shocking number of family relationships. Well might the average person conclude that there is no hope for such families.

Does anyone today speak with insight concerning the complex crisis in which the contemporary family finds itself? Who could count the number of studies conducted, courses taught and books written on the subject of the family? How blessed we are to have all this help at our fingertips! Or are we? While it seems we ought to be riding high on the waves of this vast sea of helpful information, many families appear to be drowning. Information abounds, but often we end up feeling more confused and hopeless and frustrated.

Against this tidal wave of data stands the writer of the book of Proverbs. Cutting through all the complexity, he suggests that there are two essential components in the formation of strong families: solid marriages and effective parenting. We can make it more complicated than that if we want to, but when all is said and done, if we focus on these two requirements we can transform the confusion, hopelessness and frustration that mark many families into a focused pursuit of positive change.

Till death do us part

The key passage for establishing solid marriages is summarized in Proverbs 5:18–19: 'May your fountain be blessed, and may you rejoice in the wife of your youth. A loving doe, a graceful deer – may her breasts satisfy you always, may you ever be captivated by her love.'

'May you rejoice in the wife of your youth,' says the writer, and in so saying he gives us the first qualification for solid marriages: permanence. Marriage is the bedrock upon which families are built. How can a family be strong if its foundation collapses? It can't. So the only way to strengthen the building block of society is to establish and maintain permanent marriages.

But I do not say this lightly. Lynne and I have never hidden the fact that our marriage requires a tremendous amount of work – more than many marriages do. We have been married for nearly two-and-a-half decades, and still it seems we have to struggle for every tiny step of progress we make on the path toward marital joy. Personal hurts, personality differences and the pressures of a highly visible lifestyle increase our challenges. But we pray, we talk, we seek advice, we discipline ourselves, we grow, we change, we compromise, we apologize, we confess, we adjust our expectations, we remind ourselves of our commitment, we look to the future, and we refuse to give up. We are in this marriage for life – we have chosen to stay with the spouse 'of our youth' – and we thank God for each step that brings us closer to rejoicing.

Why do we keep working at it? Because we know that in order to forge a strong family we need to establish a solid marriage. It would be wonderful if *solid* always meant 'easy and happy', but sometimes it doesn't. Sometimes *solid* means 'solidly committed, solidly persevering, solidly striving for the goal'.

Is it worth it? We think it is. Our family recently spent three days in California celebrating the graduation of our daughter, Shauna. Together we worked to finish the last-minute details for a huge graduation party, together we greeted and entertained new and old friends, together we ended the weekend with a Mother's Day brunch in our hotel, together we said our emotional farewells before Todd went back to college to finish the academic year, Shauna began her cross-country drive home and Lynne and I flew back to Chicago. What did each of us carry with us as we left? A treasure of family memories. Perhaps for us, those memories are all the more precious because they have not come cheaply.

The only kind of marriage the writer of Proverbs understands is a lifelong marriage. He would patiently listen to all the current banter about no-fault divorces and serial marriages, and then he would say again, 'Rejoice in the spouse of your youth. When you get married, stay married. Make compromises. Get help. Work at it. Fast, pray, try and try and try again. Do whatever you have to do to stay together. Make the most out of your marriage. There is no other way. Solid marriages are the key to strong families.'

Meeting in the middle

But the writer of Proverbs doesn't just tell us to stay together. He complicates the matter by telling us to rejoice! 'Don't just grin and bear it,' he says. 'Don't settle for a mere detente or even for a peaceful coexistence. Go for more than that. Find joy in your marriage!' As if that weren't enough, he paints a picture of sexual passion ('May her breasts satisfy you always') and even a deep and lasting emotional bond ('May you ever be captivated by her love'). It sounds great. But how do we get there from here?

We get there by building on every foot of common ground we can find. Every common interest. Every common value. Every common goal. Every common pleasure. Every common recreational pursuit. Every common involvement in ministry. If we have none of these in common, then we compromise, we change, we grow, we develop in new directions until we do have something in common.

Lynne and I both love to go to our family cottage in Michigan, but once we get there, our natural tendency is to head off in different directions. There is nothing I would rather do than spend time in a boat – for hours. There is nothing Lynne would rather do than walk on the beach – for miles. Both those activities are great for us as individuals; they refresh and renew us. But they do tend to separate us.

So on a regular basis Lynne gives up the serenity of the beach for the pounding of a powerboat or the rocking and rolling of a sailing boat. Though Lynne genuinely enjoys sailing, she has to work quite hard to appreciate my recent interest in powerboating, but she is making the effort.

Exchange is no robbery, so I walk on the beach with her. I still tend to see walking as a purposeful activity directed towards a particular destination, but I am beginning to see some sense in Lynne's claim that the walk itself is the destination.

While Lynne is learning to appreciate the excitement of speed, the matchless (to me, anyway) thrill of two engines in perfect harmony and the beauty of a hand-waxed hull, I am learning to appreciate the sensation of sun-warmed sand on bare skin, the graceful sway of beach grass, the lonely call of seagulls and the gentle lapping of waves at my feet. Not bad lessons for either of us to learn!

Clearly Lynne and I come at life from nearly opposite directions. Though we are compatible in most of the major areas discussed in the previous chapter, when it comes to matters of personality, we could hardly be more different. This is not uncommon for married couples. Despite the desire that most of us have to share life deeply and broadly with our spouses, many of us end up marrying opposites . . . and ultimately wishing we hadn't.

What often drives this 'opposites attract' tendency is a subconscious pull toward wholeness. In a person who is different from us we see personality traits that seem to complement or balance our personalities. We see strengths that counteract our weaknesses. We see qualities of character that we would like to have. We see someone whose 'oppositeness' will make us rounded and complete personalities.

The desire for wholeness is good. But this is how it often works itself out when opposites attract. Let's say that cool-headed, logical, mathematical Tom falls head over heels in love with free-spirited, feeling-oriented, poetry-loving Betsy. Betsy's spontaneity and emotional intensity free Tom to feel less rigid and more tuned into the childlike side of life. His caution and practicality make Betsy feel less out of control, less extreme and more grown up. So they go to the altar in a rush, believing that their differences will serve them both well.

Six months later they look at each other and say, 'We are opposites, but we are certainly not attracting.' The romantic flame that had been fuelled by their mutual desire for wholeness has been doused by the polarization caused by their differences. Why did this happen?

Let's go back to the beginning to answer that question. Tom and Betsy were attracted to each other out of a desire for wholeness. That desire is good; wholeness is good; joining up with a person who can help us achieve wholeness is good. But what they did not realize is that the only way another person's opposite characteristics can help us achieve wholeness is if we incorporate those characteristics into ourselves, if we learn from our spouses and try to take on the characteristics in them which balance our own.

Unfortunately, most of us do not even know we should be striving for that kind of wholeness within ourselves. We have bought into the charming but erroneous notion that it is enough to go through life as one half of a whole, the whole being the marriage itself.

So each partner fulfils the unique responsibilities of his or her respective half. He provides the logic; she provides the emotion. Or she provides the stability; he provides the spontaneity. Or he provides the seriousness; she provides the fun. The longer they each commit themselves to making their unique contributions to the whole the more settled and extreme they become in their opposite positions, to the point where they begin to irritate each other – and their complementary characteristics lead to polarization.

This does not have to happen. But the only way to avoid it is to give up our romantic notions of the beauty of opposites and strive for individual wholeness. We need to learn from one another and incorporate one another's strengths into our own lives. How much better for Tom and Betsy if they would each strive to be logical yet fully alive emotionally, stable and yet free to be spontaneous, serious and yet able to loosen up and have fun.

Lynne and I are both extreme people. That is why it is so hard for us to be married to each other but why we are also good for each other. In life outside marriage Lynne and I can enjoy people who are quite different from us, but we are free to take those relationships only so far. When they start getting uncomfortable we can back off, we can escape, we can avoid the discomfort. But there is no backing off in marriage, no escape, no avoiding issues. In marriage we are forced to confront each other and ourselves, we are forced to compromise, we are forced to grow – or be miserable. And like it or not, whatever forces us to grow is good.

Proverbs 27:17 says, 'As iron sharpens iron, so one man sharpens another.' The same can be said of spouses. Being married to someone as sensitive and emotionally deep as Lynne has definitely sharpened me. It has challenged me to stretch my own capacity for sensitivity and emotional depth, which has greatly enhanced my effectiveness as a leader, a pastor, a friend and a father. Being married to someone as goal-oriented and disciplined and determined as I am has similarly sharpened Lynne by challenging her to use her gifts constructively and to find practical outlets for her insights and creativity.

We went into marriage thinking we would each make great halves of the whole. We didn't realize that the task before us was to grow to the point where we could each bring wholeness to the marriage. Nor did we realize that marriage provides the university-level course in life and personal growth, and is the tool that God uses in our lives to lead us towards wholeness.

Years ago Lynne and I wrote a book on marriage called *Fit to Be Tied*. Perhaps we might better have titled it *Tied to Be Fit*. We have not yet arrived at the goal, but clearly our marriage is slowly making us fit – fit in the sense of adequate, competent, healthy, mature, balanced, godly, whole.

And what are we discovering? That whole people have a way of stumbling upon mutual joy, even if they are very different. Why? Because whole people are willing to try new activities. Whole people are willing to embrace new ideas. Whole people are willing to learn new skills. Whole people are willing to work hard. Whole people are open to new friends. Whole people dare to face challenges. Whole people have the courage to speak the truth. Whole people are not afraid to take the risks of loving. Whole people can bend without breaking and compromise without being untrue to themselves. Whole people can meet in the middle and embrace what they find there . . . and together, they can rejoice!

Keep investing

But even then, even when couples reach the point of being able to rejoice together – or if they are among those rare couples who find it easy to rejoice together from the beginning – even then they cannot get careless about working on their marriage. Every marriage requires vigilant attention and effort. I wish someone had told us almost twenty-five years ago when we got married that one of the most important things we could do was to commit ourselves to a marriage enrichment programme the day we returned from our honeymoon.

During the past two-and-a-half decades, I and other Willow Creek pastors have married hundreds of couples and watched them head off into life together. Of all these marriages, the ones that I have seen flourish have shared one common feature: both partners have made huge investments of time and energy in the marriage. As couples, they have committed themselves to regular nights out, frequent meals together and weekend breaks. Most of them have deliberately developed common recreational interests. Others have read and discussed books and articles on marriage and have listened to tapes on marriage. Some have attended marriage enrichment weekends. Many have joined small groups dealing with marital development and have discovered the tremendous benefit of gleaning insight from other couples who are as committed as they are to marital growth.

If every great marriage is the result of genuine and sustained investment by both partners, none of us can justify laziness. Yet I have seen wonderful relationships deteriorate and die out of sheer neglect. How tragic for partners to end up in the divorce court because they have failed to nurture, enhance and breathe life into the relationship that was once so precious to both of them.

Get help quickly

I recently talked with a woman who had just come from there – from the divorce court, that is. The story she related to me was as predictable as the setting sun. 'We started drifting apart,' she said. 'I knew something was wrong, but my husband didn't want to talk about it, so I pretended things were all right. But after ten years of increasing remoteness and coldness, something inside me just died. His refusal to talk, I now realize, was the beginning of the end.'

So another painful divorce and a few more children thrown out into the world wondering if mothers and fathers ever stay together any more. What might have happened if ten years ago, at the first hint of trouble, that woman had said to her husband, 'Oh, no, you don't. Not here, not in this home, not in this relationship. We are not going to give up without an attempt to make this relationship work. We are not going to let ourselves drift apart. We are going to admit that we need help right now, and we are going to get it'? What might have happened if they had gone to their parents, to trusted friends, to church leaders or to a Christian counsellor and said, 'We have hit a rough patch in our marriage. Will you help us through it? Will you give us some advice?'

When a couple's marital difficulties are addressed early on, the probability of healing the relationship is high. Probably it was not that long ago that the partners stood at the altar, lovingly gazing into each other's eyes and longing more than anything else in the world to live life together. Even if the love that initially drew them into that mutual longing has been buried beneath a lot of careless words, hurt feelings, unresolved conflicts and hidden hostilities, it can most likely be uncovered if couples get help soon. So don't wait. If you are aware of even the slightest hint of trouble in your marriage, get help now. Then you can get back to the business of enjoying your relationship and making it strong enough to provide a solid and stable environment for your children.

The scarlet letter

Before we go any further, I need to address a problem that the book of Proverbs recognizes as one of the major threats to solid marriages: the sin of adultery. Knowing that adultery cuts the heart out of many marriages and families, the writer speaks as straightforwardly as possible. 'But a man who commits adultery lacks judgment; whoever does so destroys himself. Blows and disgrace are his lot, and his shame will never be wiped away' (6:32–33).

Adultery is such an utterly destructive activity, says the writer, that anyone who engages in it lacks sense. What sensible person would do something that leads to hostility and shame and destroys spouses and children in two sets of families? It makes no sense, says the writer, so don't do it! Take it off your list of options. Consider it out of the question.

The writer feels so strongly about the destructive potential of adultery that he even warns about the danger of inappropriate flirtation. This is not a blanket prohibition of cross-gender friendships. This passage should not be used to create suspicion in society or in the church regarding friendships between couples or within groups. Nor is it a legalistic condemnation of the innocent cross-gender banter that comes in the category of legitimate fun. But . . . when it comes to the kind of seductive flirtation that can lead to sexual sin or adultery, Proverbs again minces no words. Flirtation can be deadly!

Proverbs warns a young man about the seductive ploys of a woman who is tempting him to commit adultery. The passage could also apply to a man engaging in seductive behaviour. '"So I came out to meet you; I looked for you and have found you! I have covered my bed with coloured linens from Egypt. I have perfumed my bed with myrrh, aloes and cinnamon. Come, let's drink deep of love till morning; let's enjoy ourselves with love! My husband is not at home; he has gone on a long journey. He took his purse filled with money and will not be home till full moon." With persuasive words she led him astray; she seduced him with her smooth talk. All at once he followed her like an ox going to the slaughter, like a deer stepping into a noose till an arrow pierces his liver, like a bird darting into a snare, little knowing it will cost him his life' (7:15–23).

Nowadays the offer of coloured linens and a bed perfumed with myrrh might be traded for a fire in the fireplace and a bottle of wine. The point is, the woman was painting for the young man the most seductive picture she could paint, boldly suggesting that they make love throughout the night, and clinching her argument with the revelation that her husband would be gone for a long time.

She offers the bait and he bites. But in the end, according to Proverbs, 'it will cost him his life'.

What is the warning? 'Caution! Extreme danger!' Entering into careless conversations is bad enough. But if you add a seductive setting, a weak moment and the wrong person, you will be placing yourself on an almost certain path toward a sexual sin with the potential to destroy marriages, families and lives.

Strong families can only be built upon the foundation of solid, permanent, loving marriages. We must therefore steer clear of anything that imperils or undermines marriage. We cannot afford to be naive regarding the power of temptation and seduction, even for those in strong marriages. 'So, if you think you are standing firm,' the apostle Paul writes in 1 Corinthians 10:12, 'be careful that you don't fall!' None of us is beyond being tempted. This is particularly true with respect to adultery because rarely does the reality of marriage measure up to the fantasy that a seducer promises. But we cannot forge a strong family on the foundation of a fantasy. Only the reality of a marriage based on mutual commitment, individual wholeness and growth in relationship provides a foundation strong enough to support the building of a family.

After being a pastor for more than two decades, I have lost count of the number of times I have sat with wayward husbands or wives who have wept in an extreme, heart-breaking way that you have to hear to appreciate. Almost every time they have said, 'I have wrecked everything because of what I have done. If only I could turn the clock back. If only I could make a different choice.'

No matter how unsatisfying or painful your marriage is, or how much seemingly irreparable damage it has sustained, adultery is never the answer. Even if you believe your marriage was ill-advised from the beginning, and even if it has never come close to providing you with what you hoped and dreamed it would – even then adultery is not a justifiable or constructive option.

Adultery will not reduce your pain; it will eventually and inevitably multiply it. It will add deceit and betrayal to the volatile mixture of marital disappointments you are already experiencing. And when adultery comes out into the open, as it almost always does, the shock and shame will be so much worse than you anticipated. No matter how much you are suffering in your marriage, adultery is not the answer.

There are always other answers, even for people in intense marital pain. Marriage counselling, separately or together, is the first option; even if the goal of a satisfying marriage cannot be reached soon – or perhaps ever – counselling can help individuals learn how to live fulfilling lives even within the context of a marriage that is not working as well as they would hope. Other options are to go more deeply into one's relationship with God and with friends and relatives, and to become more involved in church activities or recreational pursuits. All of these are reminders that marriage is just one dimension of life; it is not the whole of life. It is possible to create a rich and joyful life even in the midst of marital disappointments.

A wise counsellor can also help partners to readjust their expectations. Many of us go into marriage with unrealistic expectations; in some cases, no human being could ever live up to the standards we have established. Others of us have reasonable expectations but they are not realistic for the particular personality combination in our marriage. Instead of aiming for the ideal marriage of our dreams – or even for the enviable marriages we may see some of our friends enjoying – we have to decide to do the best we can with the realistic potential that exists in our marriage.

In a badly wounded marriage, a period of separation is sometimes a necessary step in the healing process. The Bible teaches that in some extreme cases divorce may be permitted because of immorality or desertion, but even then, the days leading toward a divorce will be much more endurable without the additional trauma of adultery.

For some of you, reading the past few pages may have been extremely uncomfortable because you have committed adultery or have been through a divorce. You are burdened by memories filled with pain and regret. To you I would like to offer a reminder that at the heart of Christianity is a God of grace who offers a second chance to moral failures like you and me, a God who says, 'I know you stepped over the line. I know you made some stupid mistakes. I know you sinned. But you can find grace and forgiveness at the cross. And you can walk from this day forward in purity and obedience.' As Christians we honour a Christ who came not to condemn us but to save us and to set us on a course that leads to fullness of life, peace and joy.

I call this chapter on marriage 'Forge strong families' because a thriving husband–wife relationship is an essential foundation for the entire family. It is the first requirement for establishing a home in which children can grow in all the ways God intends. Faced with what seem to be overwhelming marital challenges, many people today attempt to redefine and restructure the family unit. But does anyone really have a better idea than God's idea of a mother and a father living in loving harmony and creating a safe and stable home for their children?

If that is the best goal, shouldn't we pull out all the stops in aiming for that? Some of us will have to work harder than we ever dreamed; all of us will discover that there are no short cuts to marital growth. It almost always takes more time, more sacrifice, more tears, more compromise, more prayer, more humility and more maturity than we anticipate. It requires us to act like adults when we would rather behave like spoilt children, to learn to look at the world through another person's eyes when we would rather cling to our familiar perceptions and to stay engaged in a continuing process when everything in us wants to give up.

Stiff challenges? Yes, but we must face them. What we as parents do with our marriages will deeply affect our children. None of us will hit the bulls-eye and create a perfect union, but don't we owe the children we have brought into the world our most determined efforts? Don't we owe them the best parenting partnerships possible? The greater the security between husband and wife, the greater the security children will have in their relationships with their parents, with their siblings, with themselves and with God.

A solid marriage is where we begin as parents. But we also need specific help in parenting effectively. Proverbs has much to say about that as well, and so the theme of forging strong families is continued in the next chapter as we consider how we can relate constructively to our children.

9
Forge strong families:
Part two

I have met many people for whom life is not working well. It is not that they are not clever or that they do not try hard. Life is not working for them because they were raised by foolish parents who did not understand the delicate balances of wise parenting, who did not know how to guide them systematically and lovingly from dependence to independence, from irresponsibility to responsibility, from childishness to maturity, who did not model the virtues necessary to ensure a stable life and a productive future. At the beginning of this book I asked, and I ask again, What price do you suppose these now grown-up children would be willing to pay to be raised again by a wise mother or father?

I have met many other adults for whom life is working well, not because they never face difficulties, challenges, heartaches or disappointments but because they have the inner resources necessary to live life effectively no matter what it brings. More often than not these people attribute much of their ability to keep their daily lives running smoothly to the blessing of being raised by wise parents. And they would not trade anything for that gift. I know how they feel. My father died more than twenty years ago, but the legacy of wisdom that he left me serves me well every day.

The gift of a wise father is equalled only by the gift of a wise mother. Proverbs 31:28–29 says of the wife and mother who 'speaks with wisdom' and offers 'faithful instruction' that 'her children arise and call her blessed; her husband also, and he praises her: "Many women do noble things, but you surpass them all."' Those who have grown up under the umbrella of parental wisdom will tell you that its value far surpasses that of gold.

But there is another side to this story: the matchless joy of a wise parent who in turn watches his or her children grow up and walk in paths of wisdom.

Years ago I realized that it did not matter to me whether my children would grow up to live in big houses or have large incomes or enjoy social successes. But it mattered greatly to me that they would grow up to walk in God's wisdom and pursue his will in every dimension of their lives. Proverbs 15:20 says, 'A wise son brings joy to his father,' and I wanted to be able to experience that kind of joy.

A mutual blessing

Not long ago I had the opportunity to visit my children in California, where they were attending college. I had not seen them for six weeks, which was the longest I had been separated from them since their births. After finishing a speaking engagement on the West Coast, I met them and a group of their friends for dinner.

While we ate, I overheard one of Todd's friends ask him what he was doing the following weekend. 'I'm going down to Los Angeles,' Todd told him. 'I'm helping a friend of mine start some youth work, the same kind as we had at church when I was growing up. There are some great young people at a church down there. It's really great helping them create a group where they can learn and grow as Christians and where they can bring their un-churched friends to hear about Christ.'

Later in the evening I overheard Shauna inviting one of her friends to a Bible-study group she was involved in. Then she and another friend discussed some of the decisions they had recently made about better ways to use their free time and spend their money and discipline their minds.

I was so blessed by what I had heard that I excused the three of us from the larger group and suggested that we go outside and take a walk around the block. With one arm around each of my children, I said, 'I am teaching this weekend from the book of Proverbs. One of the verses I'm using says, "Wise children make their parents glad." You need to know that I am overflowing with gladness tonight because of the ways in which you are learning to walk in wisdom. You are fantastic children, and I am so proud of you!'

I do not mean to imply that my children are perfect or that I agree with every decision they make.

On the night of which I just wrote, one of them displayed a new tattoo of which I was not all that fond. (The other had long ago displayed one – or was it two?)

'I'm sure it won't be an issue in heaven,' they both assured me.

'You may be right,' I conceded, 'but between now and then it's a major one!'

'Relax, Dad!'

'All right, all right!'

Tattooed or not and relaxed or not, children and parents who walk in the paths of wisdom bring great joy to one another. Proverbs 17:6 says that 'children's children are a crown to the aged, and parents are the pride of their children'. All too often in our culture parents and children become adversaries; we almost come to expect that. But God had in mind an entirely different family scenario, one in which parents and children are allies in life and are genuinely proud of each other.

'Spare the rod and spoil the child' may be the most famous of the Bible's proverbs (a paraphrase of 13:24), but teaching on discipline is only a small part of the parenting wisdom offered in Proverbs. As is stated in the margin notes in *The Student Bible*, 'The overwhelming emphasis of Proverbs is on verbal encouragement and teaching. The whole book is framed as a father's words to his son (1:8 "Listen, my son, to your father's instruction") ... Mother has equally important words (1:8 "and do not forsake your mother's teaching") ... The parent–child conversation is a warm one.'

What are the necessary ingredients for warm

conversations between parents and children and for family relationships marked by a mutual sense of pride? Proverb after proverb places responsibility for such relationships on both parents and children. Children are called to 'heed the instructions' and 'listen to the knowledge' and 'accept the discipline' and 'follow the wisdom' of their parents. At a point in history where disrespect between generations is at an all-time high, this is no small challenge; it is almost counter-cultural to expect young people to go against the trend and look to their elders as models.

Many young people would say their elders have given them no reason to look up to them. In some cases such a statement is a shallow excuse for disrespect. In all too many cases, however, it is true. Few parents seem willing to rise to the challenge of the kind of parenting outlined in Proverbs, and a challenge it is – a daunting one. We as parents are called to dispense practical instructions for effective living, provide knowledge about how the world works, offer loving and balanced discipline, and both teach and model eternal virtues, life-affirming values and wisdom that is timeless.

How many parents do you know who have made it a priority to acquire these non-material gems? How many parents do you know who have taken the time to pass them on to their children? What would it take to do this? Fewer hours devoted to succeeding in business and to material gain? Fewer hours in front of the television or on the golf course? A simplified lifestyle? More hours spent around the dinner table as a family? The disciplines of reading, reflecting and talking to wise people? Prayer and seeking God's will?

A good place to start is by meditating on the Proverbs I will consider in the rest of this chapter.

Love and limits

Proverbs 23:25 says, 'May your father and mother be glad; may she who gave you birth rejoice!' Make no mistake about it. Children are treasures from God – a reward from him', we read in Psalm 127:3 – and they should be treated accordingly. They should be prized and cherished. They should hear thousands of times that their parents are crazy about them. They should grow up in an environment in which expressions of love seem as natural as breathing.

One child-development expert quoted studies that indicate that people who grew up to become healthy, well-adjusted adults can almost always look back to one parent who loved them irrationally. (That was the expert's word.) People who perpetually struggle through life and do not become well-adjusted adults or become people who sink into the extremes of depression, crime or the drive to achieve usually cannot recall being irrationally loved by either parent. The researcher concluded that in order to grow up normal, every human being has to be loved abnormally.

I think the writer of Proverbs knew that the human heart needs irrational love. The word *rejoice* is not a neutral, impassive term. It implies excitement, joy and a feeling of celebration. And that is exactly the kind of emotional environment that should surround a baby who rests in its parent's arms. Or a toddler who runs up to Mum or Dad and asks for a hug. Or a young child who sits at the dining-room table and details in jumbled and excited terms the events of school that day. Or a teenager who describes his or her dreams and goals and fears. An emotional environment like that provides the foundation for a well-adjusted life.

But the writer of Proverbs never drifts into sentimentality. There is another side to rearing these little bundles of love, these gifts from God, these innocent-looking cherubs. The reality is that they have a streak of something in them that is going to make parenting an intense, character-building challenge. There are no exceptions to this rule. The parenting drama always stretches parents to the limits of human wisdom and beyond.

What is the source of this challenge? Proverbs 22:15 says, 'Foolishness is bound up in the heart of a child; the rod of discipline will remove it far from him' (NASB).

For centuries a philosophical debate has raged about whether children are born good and then learn bad habits from their parents and their environment or are born with a natural predisposition toward mischief. Proverbs 22:15 leaves little doubt which side the Bible takes in this debate. The theological conclusion is that children are born sinful.

Most parents would say that this is the conclusion they draw from their own experience too. I remember clearly when Shauna was born. The first time I looked into her eyes, I would have bet my life that she was an exception to Proverbs 22:15. I thought, *Surely there is no rebellion lurking in the*

194

heart of this little angel. Surely there is no sinister streak of trouble in her. Surely she is perfect.

But now fast-forward the video a mere two-and-a-half years. Shauna is riding her tricycle on the pavement in front of our house. Repeatedly Lynne tells her not to ride past the huge oak tree that marks the boundary of our garden; repeatedly Shauna rides past it. Finally Lynne brings Shauna up onto the veranda, kneels in front of her, looks her squarely in the eye and then says softly but firmly, 'Shauna, I do not want to smack you. But if you ride past the oak tree one more time, I will smack you. I want you to know that now. I will smack you.' Shauna holds Lynne's gaze for a few seconds, then turns round and sticks her little bottom up in the air and says, 'Well then, Mum, you might as well smack me now!'

Lynne was dumbfounded. How could her sweet, beautiful, perfect toddler act in that way? Shauna wasn't yet three years old! What would her teenage years be like? How would we survive? That day we started praying the Parents' Prayer: 'God, help! We're in over our heads! We don't have a clue what to do with this child!'

Every parent has prayed that prayer. Lynne and I happened to get the parenting alarm call a bit early, but every parent receives it eventually. What do we do when it comes? We strive to find that delicate balance between loving irrationally and establishing necessary limits. It was painfully obvious to us that Shauna needed both: love and limits.

Verses like Proverbs 23:13–14 offered us help. 'Do not withhold discipline from a child; if you punish him with the rod, he will not die. Punish him with the rod and save his soul from death.' While no form of discipline should ever do violence to a child or be administered when a parent is out of control, this passage recognizes that punishment can be a form of love and that parents who refuse to discipline their children may ruin them. Withholding the necessary discipline from our children is like sitting back and watching them head for destruction.

There is not space in this chapter to consider in detail the various forms of discipline and punishment (smacking, isolation, removing rewards, and so on), but it is important for parents to find a form that works in their family. Because of Shauna's strong will and streak of toughness, smacking was not always the most effective means of punishing or disciplining her. (When Lynne said, 'This hurts me more than it hurts you,' it was literally true. Lynne suffered far more in administering a smacking than Shauna ever did in receiving one.) But how Shauna hated to be isolated in her bedroom for five minutes! *That* made her give a second thought to her behaviour.

The basic point in this proverb is that we parents need to find appropriate ways to influence the attitudes and behaviour patterns of our children. If we don't, if we let our children grow up without limits, boundaries, consequences, responsibilities and accountability, we are guaranteeing them a lifetime of heartache and disaster.

The sin streak in the heart of every child will gradually become a dark and driving force of self-absorption and selfish ambition that will alienate him or her from others and eventually lead to ruin in every area of life, even the spiritual. That is why parents have to grapple every day with what it means to shower their children with love while simultaneously setting and enforcing limits that help to shape character, develop virtue and instil within them a sense of Christian morality.

Speaking from the experience of having brought up two children to college age, I can say that achieving this delicate balance between love and limits has been one of the greatest challenges of my life. When do we say, 'Children will be children,' and give them some leeway, and when do we say, 'That behaviour or attitude crosses the line. It must be dealt with'? When do we intervene in our children's decision-making in order to protect them from hurtful or destructive decisions, and when do we stand back and let our children learn through the hard lessons of life? When do we comfort tenderly and when do we correct forcefully? When do we encourage and when do we warn? When do we give advice and when do we listen? When do we do which?

Those questions have driven me to my knees time and time again. But I have discovered that it is not a bad place for parents to be. When we come to God with a spirit of humility and seek his wisdom, he offers us his help through Scripture, through books, through mature friends, through counsellors and through the personal guidance of the Holy Spirit.

Competence and confidence

The second passage I want to look at is Proverbs 22:6, which says, 'Train up a child in the way he should go, and when he is old he will not turn from it.' There are two levels of meaning in this proverb.

The first is a general truth about childrearing, which says that the patterns we set for children during their early years will eventually take root in their lives and become their own. In other words, if we teach our children about things such as telling the truth, compassion, kindness, respect for others, diligence and responsibility, eventually they will accept those values for themselves.

Similarly, if we help our children understand that there is a God who loves them and a Saviour who paid the price for their sin and wants to guide their lives, usually children will claim that spiritual heritage as their own. As with other proverbs, this passage is not a promise; it offers no guarantee that our children will respond to our training in this way. It is, however, a clear statement about how life generally works and what we can usually expect.

But this verse has another meaning. Many scholars believe that the writer of Proverbs was also challenging parents to help their children discover and develop their natural abilities and interests. According to this interpretation, training up a child 'in the way he should go' means helping that child discover the path in life that has been uniquely designed for him or her.

I have come to believe that beyond offering our children massive amounts of love and appropriate limits, the next greatest gift we can give them is a discerning analysis and gradual drawing out of the special abilities that God has given them. This allows our children to say at a young age, 'I am very good at this particular activity. I enjoy using these particular skills. I am competent in this particular area.' As children grow up and move out into the world, they will be attacked, insulted, criticized and undermined from many different directions. Those children who have already acquired some abilities upon which to build a sense of confidence will have a tremendous advantage when they face those verbal and psychological enemies.

Such children will also experience the invigorating pleasure of doing what they love to do. I once heard a very young child say, 'Something inside me comes alive when I paint pictures.' The mother who had encouraged the discovery and development of that passion (and had the refrigerator artwork to prove it!) was beaming in the background. She knew the joy of watching the self-esteem and confidence of her child blossom like a spring flower.

Some time ago I met an architect who was at the top of his field. When I asked him how he ended up in that field, he said, 'When I was seven years old, my father saw that I was interested in how things worked, and had the ability to make them, so he bought me every kind of building set he could find in the toy shop. Later he helped me draw up plans for a tree house and personally supervised me in building it. Then he made sure I took mechanical drawing lessons at secondary school and helped me get into architectural college. After that, I had to work hard to establish myself. But he is the one who got me started.'

I asked him if he enjoyed his work. 'It fires me up!' he said. 'Going to work feels like going out at break time. I love it every day.' Then I asked if he thought he would have been able to find the right path on his own. He said, 'Definitely not. I had never heard of architecture nor met an architect. I didn't know there was anything special about my passion for designing things. Unless my father had noticed it, I doubt if I would ever have taken it seriously.'

I asked a woman executive who heads a publishing company on the East Coast how she ended up in her career. She said that when she was a little girl, her parents noticed two things about her: that she loved books and that she was always the leader among the children in the neighbourhood. Her family used to say, 'Darling, if you're awake, you're either reading or leading. That's important for you to know. One day you'd better have a job where you can read and lead.' Today she leads a company to do with reading. How important were her parents' observations? She has built her whole life on those observations. This, to me, is a perfect example of training a child in the way she should go.

Parents, it is so important that we get this right. Doing so requires great discernment, long hours of observation and deep wisdom from God, but when we get it right and provide the wind beneath the wings of our children's abilities and interests, we have given them an invaluable gift. In helping them discover the gifts and the passions that God has put in their lives, we give them a huge blessing by nourishing their self-esteem and building their confidence.

As a result we give ourselves a huge blessing too. What do I mean by that? I mean that there is nothing more fun for parents than watching their children use their gifts and pursue their passions. Lynne and I have made some huge parenting mistakes along the way, but we have always been committed to helping our children discover this uniqueness.

When Shauna was a small child it became obvious to us that contained within the framework of her personality were two wildly different dimensions that both needed to be nurtured. First, she was a voracious reader. By the time she went to nursery school she had read the whole series of *Little House on the Prairie* books numerous times. She would sit at the dinner table reading books (if we would let her), walk along the pavement reading books, ride in the car reading books. But she was also the quintessential 'party waiting to happen'. To her, everything was an event, a celebration, an occasion, and any time a group of people came together she was determined to be at the centre of things.

But when she reached her late teenage years, she began to feel confused. She wondered which side was really her: the dedicated student? Or the party girl? She felt so relieved when we told her she was both sides, that she had manifested both sides since she was born and that she needed to keep both sides alive. Can you imagine how much fun it is for us to watch her graduate from college as an English student who loves her field of study and then leave immediately to work at a Christian camp for the entire summer, where she is the director of programming (which means, among other things, that she plans parties for hundreds of primary school children)? To watch our children grow up and realize the potential that we saw in them as children is a thrill. Yes, it requires time and careful observation, but the reward makes it all worthwhile.

A year ago Todd left a note on my desk at church. He wrote, 'Dear Dad, I want to tell you how proud I am of you.' I read that and I almost wept. Though Todd is strong, independent and confident today, when he was young he was very sensitive and fairly timid. I knew that he needed to be challenged and stretched so he would gain confidence, but I also knew he needed to be assured that he was doing a good job. So whenever I had the opportunity, I highlighted his efforts, his successes and his competence, and I constantly told him how proud I was of him. What a reward it was to hear him say the same thing back to me.

Then he wrote, 'The older I get, the more I realize why you raised me the way you did. You always challenged me. That made me more confident in myself and in Christ. This past week, I've been thinking about the many experiences I've had that other children haven't had because they were never challenged by their parents. Thanks for all the challenges. Thanks for all the love and all the encouragement you've poured into my life. I love you.'

Have I bored you with stories about my children and quotes from them? Consider yourself fortunate. Without a conscientious editor looking over my shoulder I would have bored you even more. You see, there's nothing I'd rather write about than my children, because nothing brings me greater joy than they do. Don't misunderstand me – Lynne and I have not been perfect parents, nor have we raised perfect children. But the very differences between Lynne and me which have made our marriage so challenging have served us well as parents.

Look back through this chapter and you will notice that much of parenting is about balance – between love and limits, encouragement and challenge, advising and listening, intervening and withdrawing. Together Lynne and I have called on the wisdom of God and united our individual strengths on behalf of our children in order to provide the proper balance for them. The truth is that Shauna and Todd would have been severely handicapped had they been raised by either Lynne or me alone. They needed a parenting partnership – and they still do.

I make this point not to underscore what single parents and their children already know – that their situation is not ideal – but to encourage parents to keep the welfare of their children in mind as they work toward greater unity in marriage. And on behalf of the many single parents in my church and in many other churches, I challenge the Christian community to respond to such situations with love and grace, support and encouragement. Together may we assist these parents in such a way that their children can experience the healthy balance that all children need and deserve.

And may all of us who face the challenge of parenting remember that we have constant access to divine help. He who has been our wise and loving Father since the foundation of the world is more than willing to guide us toward the love and wisdom we need to forge strong families.

10
Cultivate compassion

Every neighbourhood has one. It is someone's worst nightmare to be one. I am referring to the unfortunate child who has been selected by unofficial vote to be the butt of jokes, the object of ridicule and the victim of bullies. It is the little boy in the grey house on the corner who is smaller than all the other boys. It is the little girl in the blue house by the railway line who wears the hand-me-down clothes that never fit properly. It is the child whose ethnic background places him or her in the minority, the child who is bad at games or perhaps the child with a physical handicap. It is hard to believe how cruel children can be.

Anyway, there is always some child who pays a high price for being who he or she is. There is always someone who gets mercilessly picked on ... unless there is an advocate nearby. In some neighbourhoods – not all, by any means, but in some – there is a big lad who decides, for reasons known only to him, to come alongside and protect the little child living out the daily nightmare.

At first no one believes the protector will defend the outcast, but then one day some bullies go too far in making trouble for the little boy who lives in the grey house. Like in a film the big lad, Jason, faces up to the bullies who are picking on his new friend. 'Meddle with Jimmy', he growls, 'and you meddle with me.' The former bullies back off and whisper, 'Hang about.' Slowly they turn their heads and look at each other. Then they look back at the self-appointed protector – the really *big* self-appointed protector.

'Personally,' says the bully ringleader, 'I have always liked Jimmy. In fact, I was thinking of having lunch with Jimmy next week. And the blokes here, I think they were planning to join us. Weren't you?'

As long as the advocate is in the vicinity, Jimmy's troubles are over.

In this chapter we're considering the plight of a group of people who, for a variety of reasons, often face the same plight that Jimmy faced. They get picked on. They are treated like outcasts. They feel helpless in the face of forces that, like bullies, assail them day after day. The book of Proverbs generally refers to them as 'the poor'. Obviously that term describes those who struggle financially, socially and in their work, but it can also mean those who struggle mentally, physically, emotionally or spiritually.

The theme of this chapter is how we as Christ's followers should respond to this broad category of people described as the poor. But before we look at that I think we need to remind ourselves that the poor have a powerful advocate in their neighbour-hood, an awesome advocate who says, 'If you meddle with the poor, you meddle with me.' I am talking about God himself. Throughout the book of Proverbs, God reveals his special concern for the poor and makes it clear that he considers neglect or mistreatment of the needy as a personal affront.

'He who oppresses the poor shows contempt for their Maker,' says Proverbs 14:31, 'but whoever is kind to the needy honours God.' What does it mean to show contempt for God? It means that we are dishonouring and disgracing God or regarding him as worthless. Do you think God is going to take that lying down? God is not mocked. Those who mis-treat the poor will have to reckon with him.

God offers an equally strong promise to those who show mercy to the poor. Proverbs 19:17 says, 'He who is kind to the poor lends to the LORD, and he will reward him for what he has done.' The writer of this proverb uses the language of finances to reveal God's attitude towards those who are kind to the poor. Whenever we offer to the poor our gifts of time, treasures or talents, it is as if we are making a loan to God, and God promises to pay back the loan with plenty of interest.

This theme is repeated throughout the book of Proverbs. 'A generous man will himself be blessed, for he shares his food with the poor' (22:9). 'He who despises his neighbour sins, but blessed is he who is kind to the needy' (14:21). 'He who gives to the poor will lack nothing, but he who closes his eyes to them receives many curses' (28:27). A dozen similar passages make the same point: the God of the universe is so concerned about the plight of the poor that he promises his blessing to any of us who will respond to their needs and act on their behalf. Those of us who are indifferent or cold-hearted towards the poor can count on feeling the heavy hand of God's wrath. 'Meddle with the poor', says God, 'and you meddle with me. Bless the poor, and you will be blessed by me.'

The point is not to say, 'Do you want to be deluged with good gifts from God? Then give to the poor.' This is not about giving so we can get. This is not about discovering a lucky charm that will assure us health and wealth. This is about realizing how closely God identifies with the poor and how deeply he feels their pain. It is about realizing that if we truly want to follow God we need to care about what he cares about, let our hearts be broken by what breaks his heart and become advocates for what he advocates.

That brings us to the purpose of this chapter: to provide practical advice from the book of Proverbs about how to cultivate compassionate hearts. In other words, how can we learn to show mercy and grace to the poor? How can we break out of our selfishness or apathy? How can we expand our hearts so we are concerned about more than our own families and close friends? How can we embrace more than the little world that exists within the comfort and safety of our home? How can we develop a ministry, a career or a vocation that offers us a concrete means of serving the poor?

Opening our eyes

Part of the answer to how to cultivate a compassionate heart is hidden in the second half of Proverbs 28:27: 'He who closes his eyes to them [the poor] receives curses.' The hidden implication in those words is that the first step in opening our hearts to the poor is to open our eyes to them. We need to resist the temptation to look away. We need to choose to look into the faces of the suffering. We need to make ourselves see the everyday reality of those whose lives are badly broken.

Every person I know who has a heart of compassion can describe in graphic terms the specific time and place when his or her eyes were first opened to the needs of the poor. I remember when it happened to me. I was sixteen. My father, an eccentric Christian businessman, wanted to help me grow up. So he gave me a pile of airline tickets and sent me off alone on a two-month journey throughout Africa, the Middle East and Europe.

One of my first stops was Nairobi, Kenya. One of my first sights in Nairobi was of people dying in the streets. I can still see in my mind the bloated bellies, the rotting limbs and the fly-covered faces. I can still feel the churning in my stomach. I can still hear God's voice saying, 'This changes everything, doesn't it? Because now you have seen it.'

Until that point in my life, I had seen little real need; even the poorest part of Kalamazoo, Michigan, was a far cry from the streets of Nairobi. Abject poverty and starvation were nothing more than abstract and distant concepts to me. But when my eyes were opened to the true condition of the poor, the abstract became real and tragic and haunting.

I had a decision to make. Would I keep my eyes open, or would I close them? Would I let what I had seen fill my vision, or would I quickly look away? Would I intentionally arrange my life in order to keep the needs of suffering people at the forefront of my mind? Or would I allow a self-centred agenda to push the poor to the back of my mind where they could no longer make me feel guilty or sad or responsible, where they could no longer 'bother' me?

Whether or not we keep our eyes open determines whether or not we will grow in compassion. Expanding our hearts always starts with what we choose to see.

I once had dinner with a well-known and successful singing group that frequently performs at large events. During dinner, members of the group, who are all followers of Christ, told me about their work with inner-city children in some of America's largest and most dangerous cities. Using the money they earned through their music, they established youth clubs, teaching programmes, music and art festivals and Bible studies. In addition to financing these various projects, each member of the group works on the ground in one of their projects at least once a month.

When I finally had a chance to interrupt their enthusiastic descriptions of their various projects, I asked them why they took the time from their programme of performances to work on the ground. One member said, 'We donated our money to start these projects because there was such tremendous need. The children we work with are at risk; they basically have no hope unless someone intervenes.'

Another group member added, 'But the reason we go beyond financial involvement is because we need to see these children at first hand. We need to be reminded every month of what real life is like for a lot of real children. It is too easy for us to get caught up in our own lives and forget.'

A third member continued, 'We don't want to become like so many other music groups that drift into narcissistic oblivion because they care only about themselves and the size of their next gig. We want to care about other people and about real needs, but we won't do it if we isolate ourselves in our own little world.'

What were they doing? They were intentionally arranging their schedules in such a way that they had to keep their eyes open to the plight of the poor. What was the result? Their hearts were growing bigger. They were cultivating compassion.

Have you opened your eyes to the world beyond your safe and comfortable existence? Is your heart growing because of what you are seeing? When you ask yourself honestly if you are more compassionate now than you were five years ago, what do you discover?

It is not difficult to open our eyes to the poor, the needy, the weak, the oppressed, the neglected. There are many ways to begin seeing. We can visit a local nursing home and sit in the dining room for half an hour; go to a local hospital and peer through the windows of the intensive-care baby unit at the sick babies wired up to machines; park our cars outside a Crisis at Christmas centre and watch the hungry people who pass through the doorway; walk with a friend through the streets of an inner-city area; visit a drug rehabilitation centre or a ward for AIDS patients. Even a more thoughtful reading of the newspaper can open our eyes to needs and concerns we typically ignore.

At Willow Creek we frequently take groups of fifty or sixty adults into Chicago for Vision Trips specifically designed to open the eyes of our suburban church members to the plight of the inner-city poor and our partners who directly serve them. On the bus ride into the city a leader from our Extension Ministries describes the various projects with which we are involved. Throughout the day, group members have the opportunity to visit a number of these projects. What happens to these people when they stand on the pavement in poor inner-city areas and open their eyes to the need? More often than not they hear the words I heard on a pavement in Nairobi: 'This changes everything, doesn't it? Because now you have seen it.' And they know that this is true.

Extending our hands

Opening our eyes inevitably makes our heart begin to swell with the seeds of compassion, but what cultivates that seed is to touch the poor personally through acts of practical service. Proverbs 31:20 describes a person of compassion as one who 'opens her arms to the poor and extends her hands to the needy'.

One of the most famous men in the world has long been extending his hands in service to the poor. Ten years ago Paul Newman started a food company called 'Newman's Own'. Since then he has poured eighty million dollars of the profits into hundreds of charities.

I recently read an article about the camp Newman started for children diagnosed with cancer. Periodically he visits the camp and stations himself at a little lemonade stall and pours out lemonade for these desperately sick children. When asked by a journalist why he does that, he shrugged and said, 'Well, I guess because I love doing it.' It sounds to me like writing cheques for charities and pouring out lemonade has expanded his heart.

I read a similar article about a man from my own church who came up with a creative way of serving the poor. After volunteering for a week in the Dominican Republic, where he helped to build a house for a homeless family, he decided to begin importing the coffee beans that some of the peasants were growing behind their huts in a Spanish district. His little business is helping to provide these hard-working men and women with stable incomes so they can feed their families, and it is helping to stimulate their local economy. What motivates him to pour his time and energy into this venture is the knowledge that every pound of coffee he imports and sells represents a potential blessing to a Dominican family.

There are Christian men and women with expertise in business, marketing, importing, nutrition, education, economics, banking, retailing, and every other field. More often than not all that expertise is devoted solely to profit-making. What would happen if Christians around the world began to think creatively about how they could use their expertise, resources, opportunities, networks, products, influence and power to improve the lives of the poor? Think about you, your family or your company. What possibilities do you see?

There are so many options for serving. In the United States, many colleges have teaching programmes for inner-city children; others offer opportunities for work in the Third World during vacations. Most communities have canteens and shelters for the homeless that use volunteer staff. Habitat For Humanity uses skilled and unskilled volunteers to help build affordable housing for the deserving poor. Prison Fellowship uses volunteers to minister in prisons. Organizations such as Youth For Christ, Youth With a Mission, Young Life and InterVarsity Christian Fellowship offer opportunities to serve young people in need. Organizations for retired people often seek volunteers for a variety of projects, as do many denominations.

Many individual churches also have projects similar to those at Willow Creek, offering church members opportunities to serve the poor by helping to renovate blocks of flats, teach schoolchildren, care for the children of teenage mothers, stock the shelves of charity shops that provide low-cost goods for poor families or offer some other form of hands-on service as a wonderful means of expressing the compassion that is growing in their hearts.

Other people, like our coffee-bean importer,

express compassion by signing up for week-long projects in the Dominican Republic or at an orphanage in the Baja region of Mexico. Still others do so by helping out closer to home. Some at our church serve the families of children with special needs. Parents of these children can rarely attend church because they can never leave their children unattended, nor can they put them in an ordinary Sunday-school class. So a group of volunteers meets in a room at church and provides one-to-one care for these children while their parents attend the church service.

Undoubtedly there are similar opportunities to serve in your country and in your church – and they don't have to fit within a structured project. What about the widows in your church? Or young families struggling with the continuing illness of a parent or a child? Or single mothers trying to hold down jobs and get transport and cook meals and read bedtime stories? All of these people, and so many others, could benefit tremendously from simple acts of compassion offered by people like you and me.

Recently one of my friends was buying groceries for her family. She was hurrying because she had guests coming for dinner, so she was frustrated when she discovered she had ended up in a slow-moving queue. She looked to the front of the queue and saw a woman rummaging through her purse; then the checkout lady shouted, 'What do you mean, you don't have any money?' My friend's first thought was, *Why do I always pick the wrong queue? Doesn't she care that I'm in a hurry?* Everyone else in the queue behind her began complaining.

But then my friend felt God tugging at her heart suggesting that she pay the woman's bill! 'But, God,' she said, 'you know I hate giving up my money. And I don't think my husband will understand. Besides that, I . . .' Then she looked at the woman – at her worn-out look and her shabby clothes – and she imagined the children who might be waiting for the woman at home. Then she thought about all that God had done for her. Smiling, she leaned over to the checkout lady and quietly said, 'Can you add my groceries to hers, and I'll pay for it all.'

My friend said she felt like she was floating as she drove home. In an unplanned and unpretentious way, she had opened her eyes and extended her hand, and God had blessed her with joy. I can't read that story without tears coming to my eyes. The opportunities are all around us and God's Spirit is whispering, 'Go for it. Do it. Offer compassion.' All we have to do is respond.

The joy of giving

Yesterday I had to write the cheques for our household bills and send both my children money to help towards their monthly college expenses. It was an emotional experience for me. Parting with cash always makes me sad. I can't help it; I'm Dutch from head to toe. But there are three kinds of cheque that are never hard for me to sign, even as a Dutchman, three kinds of cheque I love to write.

The first is our family tithe, a cheque that we make out to Willow Creek Community Church at the end of every month. Leviticus 27:30 tells us that 'a tithe of everything from the land, whether grain from the soil or fruit from the trees, belongs to the LORD; it is holy to the LORD'. In Malachi 3:10 God says, 'Bring the whole tithe into the storehouse, that there may be food in my house.' Numerous passages in the New Testament (Matthew 6:19–34; 19:16–30; Luke 12:13–34; 16:1–15; Acts 2:44–45; 4:32–37; 2 Corinthians 9:6–15; 1 Timothy 6:17–19, and others) suggest a much broader view of giving and make it clear that we are to view all our resources as God's and to share them generously according to our means. Nonetheless the leadership of our church holds to the traditional Christian view that the tithe represents the minimum amount that Christians should give to the work of God as it is carried out through a local body of believers.

For me, therefore, sending the tithe is a means of honouring God and furthering his work of redemption. It is also a way for me to thank him for a healthy mind and body, for a place to work, for people I love to work with and for an income that allows me both to care for my own family and to respond to needs within the larger family of God.

Whenever I sign that cheque, I enjoy the additional knowledge that part of the money goes to projects which help the poor. Part of it is invested in the lives of needy people in Chicago, in Mexico, in the Dominican Republic and elsewhere around the world. Recently I read a report regarding the various Willow Creek projects that serve the poor, and I almost started crying. I was so grateful for these opportunities to honour God and expand my heart by giving to the poor.

Another cheque I love to write supports a child in

a Third-World country through World Vision. I am sure that many of you write similar cheques each month to parachurch organizations that feed and clothe and house the poor. It is only right and fitting that we should do this. James 2:15–16 says, 'Suppose a brother or sister is without clothes and daily food. If one of you says to him, "Go, I wish you well; keep warm and well fed," but does nothing about his physical needs, what good is it?' In addition, 1 John 3:17–18 says, 'If anyone has material possessions and sees his brother in need but has no pity on him, how can the love of God be in him? Dear children, let us not love with words or tongue but with actions and in truth.' Who is our 'brother or sister' in need? It can be any one of God's created children who has fallen on difficult times or has faced loss or tragedy. We can't help every person in need. But there are many needs we can and should meet.

The third cheque I love to write is one that Lynne and I place in the offering plate each year at our Christmas Eve service. Along with many other families, we have established a tradition of giving a Christmas gift, above and beyond our regular tithes and offerings, to a fund that goes almost exclusively to the poor. There is no offering our church treasurers are more excited to add up than the Christmas Eve offering. It is always a heart-enlarging experience when our congregation celebrates together the amount of that offering and the individuals, churches and projects to which it will be dispersed. We always sense God's affirmation and favour.

What song, Frances?

The third way to cultivate a heart of compassion is to build loving relationships with the poor. Once we open our eyes and then extend our hands in service or giving, our hearts will start to enlarge. But nothing will nourish a compassionate heart better than establishing personal relationships with those in need.

My father spent nearly every Sunday afternoon for twenty-five years leading a little sing-song for a hundred forgotten, poor women with learning difficulties at the local hospital. It was something he felt called by God to do, and I am sure that if he were alive he would still be doing it. Recently I was reflecting on what sustained that consistent flow of compassion from a tough, high-powered, globe-trotting businessman. What kept his heart soft through all those years?

I think a big part of it was that he had got to know those women personally. He wrote plenty of cheques to meet certain needs they had, and knowing that his money increased their well-being brought him a great joy. But what kept his heart continually expanding and what kept him seeking new ways to serve them was that to him those women had become individuals with personalities and life stories worth caring about and honouring.

Occasionally he would drag me to one of these services. I would listen while he asked if any of the women had a particular song she would like the group to sing. When any woman raised her hand, he would call her by name. 'Frances, what song can we sing for you?' Then again, 'Joanne, which song would you like?' Then, 'Helen?' And, 'Annie?' I can still remember the names he called because I was so impressed that he knew them. At the end of every service he would stand at the back by the door and hug every one of those hundred women. Sometimes they would give him a soggy sweet or a little hand-scrawled note. At Christmas time, he bought small gifts for each of them. How could such personal involvement not nourish the compassion growing in his heart?

Recently I talked with a college student who works for an organization that initiates personal relationships between college students and persons with Down's syndrome. The organization sets up the first meeting and then the college student takes over, inviting the individual with Down's syndrome to join him or her to watch sporting events, attend social activities or participate in Bible studies. What had softened the heart of this college student and prompted him to be a spokesman for this organiza-tion was his own long-term friendship with a young man with Down's syndrome. That relationship has so affected him that he wants other people to have the same kind of heart-expanding experience.

In a recent fax, a colleague in the Dominican Republic described a meeting she had had with a group of Dominican women who are trying to estab-lish community banks that can enable them and their neighbours to invest in small businesses and thereby support their families. She hears the same stories over and over again from these women, stories of the pain and frustration of crashing into yet another wall of discrimination and injustice – the walls that so often surround the poor. On most days this staff member feels like she is fighting a losing battle in her attempts to be an advocate for women like these. But she perseveres. Why? Because she knows these women – she knows how hard they work and against what odds. Her compassion for them motivates her to keep going.

Catching the Spirit

The reason that establishing personal relationships with those in need so deeply transforms us is that doing so is a genuine 'God Thing'. I call it that because that is what God did, through Christ, when he saw us living in spiritual poverty. Look at 2 Corinthians 8:9: 'For you know the grace of our Lord Jesus Christ, that though he was rich, yet for your sakes he became poor, that you, through his poverty, might become rich.'

What this means is that Christ was so moved by compassion that he left the spiritual wealth and splendour of heaven and lived for thirty-three years on this needy, suffering planet, so that spiritually impoverished people like us could be restored to God, have our spirits enriched and be guaranteed the gift of heaven for all eternity. But he did even more than this. In living and dying among us, he offered us not only our salvation but also the incomparable gift of his friendship. 'I want to get to know you,' he said through word and deed. 'I want to extend my hand of fellowship to you. I want to walk beside you every day of your life.'

In an earlier chapter I mentioned that we tend to

become like the people with whom we walk. If we walk with foolish people, we tend to become foolish. If we walk with wise people, we tend to become wise. And if we walk with compassionate people, we tend to become compassionate. The point is obvious. If we walk closely with the Lord, we will find his love beginning to take root and grow in our hearts. We will find ourselves wanting to follow his example. We will find ourselves wanting to open our eyes to the poor, extend our hands to the poor and build relationships with the poor.

And we will not be doing this out of a mere sense of humanitarian duty but because we have truly caught the Spirit of Christ, and that spirit of self-giving love will propel us into consistently compassionate action.

11
Manage anger

People do the daftest things when they lose their tempers.

Have you ever seen toddlers throw tantrums? They wail and scream and babble all kinds of nonsense. They hurl their little bodies to the ground, their tiny arms flailing and their tiny legs kicking in the air in a comically frantic dance of raw emotion. You would think they had gone mad.

Have you ever seen a teenager lose his or her temper? I once watched one of the best athletes in my school slam his fist into his locker so hard that he broke his hand and ruined his athletic career. Had he foreseen the consequences of losing control, he probably would have stopped himself. But maybe not – his girlfriend had just jilted him and he was mad.

Have you ever seen a young mother with two small children and a husband who is never at home lose her temper? It is not a pretty sight. Pots and pans fly around the kitchen, dining-room chairs slide across the floor and, worst of all, little children get screamed at for doing the things that little children do. In her right mind, every mother knows better than to let fly, but this mother is not in her right mind – she is mad.

Have you ever seen a grown man lose control of his temper? This can be truly frightening because of the dangers posed by his power and strength when out of control. The potential damage ranges from household destruction to abuse of his wife or even to violence against his own children. With language ranging from mild profanity to strong expletives that make other people's blood run cold, he makes sure everybody knows that he is really, really mad.

Not long ago, a well-known professional basketball player physically attacked his coach – twice, as a matter of fact. The attack cost him a multi-million dollar contract and a year-long suspension from the National Basketball Association. Why did he do it? Apparently he just went mad.

In English usage, in the United States at least, we have almost come to use the words *angry* and *mad* interchangeably. It has become common for children to warn each other by saying, 'Watch out. Mum (or Dad) is mad!' Colleagues alert each other to a potential risk by saying, 'Keep your head down. The boss is mad!' Spouses push each other away by saying, 'I need some space. I'm mad!'

But are the concepts of anger and madness interchangeable? Does anger always have to manifest itself in the kind of frenzied behaviour that is destructive, dangerous, out of control, violent and, yes, sinful?

The Bible goes to great lengths to keep the two concepts, anger and madness, separate. 'Be angry,' says the apostle Paul to the Christians in Ephesus, 'but do not sin' (Ephesians 4:26 RSV). In other words, it is all right to be angry; it is all right to experience what the dictionary calls 'strong feelings of displeasure and indignation'. But it is not all right to manifest our anger in behaviour that is sinful and 'mad'; it is not all right to throw tantrums, frying pans or punches.

According to the Bible there is a way to express anger constructively, but it is not easy. Proverbs 16:32 says, 'He who is slow to anger is better than the mighty, and he who rules his spirit than he who takes a city' (RSV). I like that phrase – 'rules his spirit' – and I am glad that the writer lived in the real world of intense feelings and highly charged relationships. I appreciate his realization that sometimes it takes more strength and courage to control our emotions than it does to capture a fortified city.

I once interviewed a decorated hero of the Vietnam war. After answering my questions about his life-and-death struggles in the war, he told me about an even greater challenge he faced after returning from the war: rebuilding his badly broken marriage. He claimed that it required less courage to charge into an enemy encampment in Vietnam than it took to swallow his pride, enter marriage counselling and face the truth about himself and his ways of relating to his wife.

Have you lost your temper lately? Have you screamed irrationally at your children or even struck them in anger? Have you left your spouse or your best friend shaking from the force of your threatening words? Are you the kind of person who snaps at the bank cashier when he or she makes a mistake? Are you the kind who elbows people in crowded shops? Do you find yourself sounding your horn unnecessarily during rush-hour traffic? Have family celebrations at Easter or Christmas been ruined by your outbursts? Do you often saturate the air around you with your steaming irritability?

Ruling our spirits, says Proverbs, is better than being a mighty war hero who can capture cities. But ruling our spirits means controlling our anger. I, like you, would like to do that, but all too often I find myself falling short. Why? What is this powerful emotion called anger that seems to have such control over our thoughts, our words and our actions?

Buried beneath complexity

You and I are not the only ones who ask that question. Many psychologists consider anger our most baffling emotion. Emotions such as happiness, sadness and fear are fairly easy to understand, but anger is different.

For example, what determines the length of our fuse? Some people get angry over the slightest irritation while others face major calamities or injustices without getting angry. And what determines our means of expressing anger? Some people turn their anger inwards while others hurl it out at the people around them. What is responsible for the varied responses? Genetic differences? Early childhood experience? Spiritual maturity? The luck of the draw? A combination of all these?

From God's Word, one thing we know about anger is that God created us with the capacity to get angry. Scripture describes God's righteous anger; in passage after passage we read that 'God's anger was kindled' against sin, rebellion, evil and injustice. Psalm 30:5 says that God's 'anger lasts only a moment, but his favour lasts a lifetime'. While the psalmist was confident that God's anger is never the end of the story, he did not deny God's anger. God's anger is real and intense, a force to be dealt with. As creatures made in his image, we have that same capacity to experience strong feelings of anger.

If God himself gets angry, anger is not a bad or sinful emotion that inevitably leads to bad or sinful behaviour. Just as God's anger is righteous, so our anger can drive us to take actions that are good and right and honourable.

Some of the best decisions I have ever made have been prompted by anger. Sometimes I have got so angry with myself for my repeated mistakes, failures or sins in a particular area that I have finally taken the necessary steps to bring about a positive internal change. At other times I have felt such anger over injustices I have seen in society that I have been prompted to launch new projects at our church or to support and encourage others as they have done so. I venture to say that many wonderful, God-honouring endeavours throughout history and throughout the world have been initiated and driven by somebody's righteous anger.

The fact remains, however, that often our feelings of anger lead to behaviour that is anything but righteous. Our good judgment and our good intentions get buried under the complexity of our intense feelings, and we have no clue about how to move forward constructively. In our confusion and lack of understanding, we take actions that are decidedly destructive towards ourselves and towards others. Though I cannot in this chapter delve deeply into the emotional and spiritual complexities of anger (having neither the space nor the necessary expertise), I do want to mention some of the destructive ways that many of us deal with anger and then focus on some positive steps that have proved helpful in my own life.

Bottlers and spewers

Because we don't realize that there are better options, most of us choose one of two ways to deal with feelings of anger. Either we bottle them up or we spew them out.

Bottlers tend to deny that they get deeply upset by the hurts, disappointments and frustrations of life. They pride themselves on never getting angry. Bottlers are usually operating from the distorted belief that any feelings of anger are bad. Many bottlers were not allowed to express anger as children. As adults, they are convinced they must continue that pattern of denial and repression; they think it is good and God-pleasing. They also think it will work. They truly believe that if bad feelings are pushed down deeply enough, they will eventually go away. When it comes to anger, their motto is, 'Out of sight, out of mind.'

But they are quite wrong. Burying anger is rather like the contemporary environmental problem of burying toxic waste. When the canisters of poison are buried underground just outside the city, everybody thinks the problem is gone. But later, people on the outskirts of town start falling ill. Their strange combination of symptoms is traced back to a contaminated water system and to the buried canisters of poison that have been leaking their toxic waste for years.

Bottled-up anger always leaks, and when it does, it poisons our bodies, our minds and our relationships. It poisons our bodies in the form of headaches, stomach problems, sleep disorders and a host of other physical symptoms. It poisons our minds in the form of distorted thinking, irrationality, loss of self-esteem, confusion, cynicism, hopelessness, despair; serious depression, which can be debilitating, is an almost inevitable result of chronic internalized anger.

These negative internal conditions can't help but manifest themselves outwardly in irritability, short tempers and bad moods, which we then carry into our relationships with our spouses, children, friends, colleagues, neighbours and anyone with whom we are involved on a regular basis. Many people who try to bury anger end up sulking. When we ask sulking people what is wrong, the standard answer is, 'Nothing.' When they get tired of sulking, they often move on to other unhealthy behaviour, such as withdrawing from the relationship or trying to manipulate the other person; they will do anything but admit that they are deeply upset. 'I am not angry,' they repeat to themselves while the stench of a deadly poison continues to swirl around them.

Many bottlers are deliberate bottlers. They choose to repress their anger because they mistakenly believe that they should. There are, however, also unintentional bottlers. These people do not know that they are angry. For example, if a little girl grows up in the home of a raging, abusive parent who behaves in unpredictable or frightening ways, she will probably live in a near-constant state of fear; fear becomes the dominant emotion in her life. Even when her parent does something that would provoke anger in any clear-thinking adult or even in a healthy child, this little girl is too terrified to feel anger. The anger may be there deep inside, but her access to it is blocked by the intensity of her fear.

When she grows up, her friends lament that she never gets angry, even when she sees injustice in the world or when she is deliberately mistreated or when the welfare of her children is threatened. Like the little girl she was, she still responds to threatening circumstances with fear and loses access to the anger that could propel her into positive action. Because access to her own anger has been blocked by fear, she is unable to respond to life in a healthy, responsible, adult way.

The opposite of a bottler is a spewer. These people have no problem admitting or accessing their anger and no problem letting fly. When it comes to expressing anger, they act like a burst dam. They are not about to let bottled-up anger give them a stomach ache or put them in a bad mood. If they have to slam the door and kick the dog and curse their best friend or even God in order to let off steam, they will do it. It doesn't matter that they often leave a trail of bruised people in their wake.

The writer of Proverbs was well aware of the damage spewers can do, both in terms of the harm they cause others and of the destructive forces they set in motion. That is why he said, 'Do not make friends with a hot-tempered man, do not associate with one easily angered, or you may learn his ways and get yourself ensnared' (22:24). When we spend time with spewers, not only do we tend to get hurt, but also we tend to start spewing ourselves. Mutual spewing often leads to the out-and-out madness described at the beginning of this chapter. Proverbs tells us that only 'a fool gives full vent to his anger' (29:11). Spewers are foolish people who are not safe to be near. If we are wise, we will give them a wide berth.

A wise alternative

Though bottlers and spewers look like polar opposites, they share a common problem: neither of them gets rid of their anger. They may move it around a bit or poke a few holes in it, but when all is said and done, it is still there. Why? Because the only way to put anger behind us is to learn from it, and neither bottlers nor spewers invest the time and energy it takes to do that. So they remain stuck. Without understanding the root causes of their anger, they are destined to perpetuate a continuing cycle of anger.

'A short-tempered man must bear his own penalty,' says Proverbs 19:19. 'You can't do much to help him. If you try once you must try a dozen times!' (LB). Why does the hot-tempered spewer who vomits his anger all over everybody keep ending up in the same frenzied place? Because spewing without learning doesn't accomplish a thing.

Some time ago, a clinical psychologist in our congregation alerted me to the ill-advised trend in some counselling circles that promotes the unbridled expression of rage. People seeking release from anger are encouraged to beat pillows and swing bats and punch bags. But, according to my psychologist friend, 'studies show that the catharsis of emotion alone is not enough for genuine healing'. In some cases the unbridled, cathartic expression of rage breeds more rage. It can be a constructive process only if it leads a person back to that basic question: Why am I angry?

As we learned earlier, anger is neither good nor bad. It is an indication that something is not right. It is like the warning light on the dashboard of a car that informs us that something under the bonnet of our car needs attention. If we don't pay attention to that something, if we sit looking at the little red warning light, nothing is going to change, and that little red light is not doing us a bit of good. But if that warning light prompts us to get out the manual or lift the bonnet in order to find out what is wrong, that little red light has served us well.

So it is with anger. It serves us well if it prompts us to dig below the surface and work out exactly why we are so upset. Of course that can happen only if we recognize and acknowledge our anger. Some people may need to see a professional Christian counsellor in order to work through the issues that block access to their anger. Others of us need to become more adept at reading the indicators in our minds, our bodies and our behaviour. Maybe it is a stiffening of our posture, a clenching of our fists or a setting of our jaw. Maybe it is a rising sense of frustration, confusion, impatience or irritability. Maybe we can detect it in our tone of voice or our abrupt speech patterns. Whatever the manifestation, we need to become aware of when our emotional temperature is rising. The sooner we can realize that what is going on inside us is anger, the sooner we can begin to learn from it.

Once we have acknowledged our anger, the next step in learning to manage it is to remind ourselves that we have choices about what we do with that anger. We do not have to deny our anger and bottle it up; nor do we have to spew it forth destructively. We do have other choices.

I know that in situation comedies and movies it often appears that the only possible way to express anger authentically is to slam a door, scream obscenities, throw a punch or fire a gun. But that is Hollywood. The Bible clearly states otherwise.

Remember Proverbs 16:32, which tells us that mightier is he who rules his spirit than he who captures a fortified city. Of course it is not easy to make the right choices in the midst of anger, but it can be done. (More on this later.)

The next step in learning to manage anger is to focus on the why. Why are we angry? What are the root causes of our anger? I do not mean that we simply need to identify the external event or circumstance that prompted our anger. Most of us can easily identify that. We are usually well aware of what happened in the world around us, in our relationships or in our circumstances to make us angry.

We have no trouble making statements like these: I get angry when the single mothers in my church take their cars to local garages for repairs and get taken advantage of. Or, I get angry at my spouse when he (or she) makes financial decisions that affect my life without consulting me. Or, I am angry because my boss withholds information from me about what is going on in the company. Or, I am angry because my father never listens to me. Or, I am angry because I am stuck in a traffic jam – again! These external causes of anger are usually fairly obvious.

What we may not readily be aware of is why those particular interactions, events or circumstances produced anger in us. While our anger may be prompted by events around us, our anger is driven by something internal, by an underlying attitude (based on a certain moral judgment, belief or assumption) that has been violated by the external event. To learn from our anger we need to uncover that underlying attitude. Then we can begin to make conscious and educated choices about how to proceed.

Perhaps our choice will be to try to change a particular circumstance, to fight for a cause or overturn an injustice. Perhaps our choice will be to try to resolve a dispute with someone else. Perhaps our choice will be to learn to accept a disappointing state of affairs. Perhaps our choice will be to change one of our internal attitudes. At this level real progress in anger management is made.

What does this process look like in practice? Let's go back to the person who gets angry when single mothers are taken advantage of by car mechanics. The external event that prompted the anger is obvious. But what internal attitude might be driving that angry response? Most likely it is a noble moral judgment about how needy people should be treated. When a judgment like that is violated we ought to feel angry. We ought to experience a righteous kind of anger that pushes us into righteous action. When needy people are mistreated, there is a crusade waiting to be launched. Perhaps God will use our anger to prompt us to take up the cause.

What about the person who gets angry when a spouse makes financial decisions without discussing them? Again, the external event is obvious. But what internal attitude is being violated? Perhaps it is an assumption about who should handle the finances in a marriage. Perhaps it is a deeply held belief about communication. Perhaps it is a moral judgment about how and where money should be spent.

Without pinpointing the underlying issue, it is almost impossible to have a constructive conversation. But identifying the underlying issue allows both people to focus on pertinent issues. They may not easily come to an agreement, but at least they can focus on the real sources of conflict without getting sidetracked by incidental issues.

What underlying attitudes might be driving the person who is angry because her boss is withholding information from her, and how might she best respond? If the internal attitude being violated is her belief about how an effective organization needs to operate, there might be several ways to respond. Perhaps she needs to discuss the issue with her boss and see if different communication procedures might be instituted within the company. Perhaps she needs to find a new job in an organization in which she could accept the values which determine procedures. Or perhaps she needs to accept the fact that she works in a setting in which effectiveness is not the highest priority, and she needs to decide to do the best she can under those circumstances. If she suspects that information is being withheld for deceitful reasons, undoubtedly her moral conviction concerning the need for honesty is being violated, and she needs to confront the person doing that. Perhaps, however, she is angry because she believes she needs to be in the know to do her job. If so, she needs to examine that internal belief. Is it true? Or is that an inappropriate and self-centred attitude that she needs to change?

What about the young man who is angry because his father never listens to him? Very likely a reasonable expectation regarding father–son relationships is being violated. What constructive choices does the son have? He can try to initiate honest communication with his father. If he needs help with this process, he can seek the advice of a Christian counsellor and perhaps even ask his father to join him in meeting with a counsellor. If these options fail, he may have to go through the process of grieving that his father refuses to engage in an authentic relationship. This is not easy, but sometimes there is no other constructive response to anger than the slow process of working through grief and coming to accept a state of affairs that we cannot change. Again, this is not an easy option, but if we refuse to take it, we are destined to live a life dominated by anger and its destructive consequences.

But I deserve . . .

What about those of us who get angry when we get stuck in traffic jams? This last illustration is an example of what I call circumstantial anger. It has nothing to do with injustice in the world. It is not a result of someone mistreating us or taking advantage of us. It is about impersonal and unavoidable circumstances that encroach to varying degrees upon our comfort, our convenience, our agenda, our goals, our preferences, our schedule, our perceived rights or our general good in some way. And often this encroachment makes us angry.

This form of anger is common today because of the narcissistic attitudes so prevalent in our culture. In many of the self-help books based on pop psychology and in the meditation exercises promoted by some contemporary philosophies and religions, we discover an attractive but false view: that we are the centre of the universe and that what we want or need is the most important thing in the world. Too often today the healthy kind of confidence and self-esteem that God intends for us to have is distorted into an unhealthy egoism. The healthy boundaries required for sane living and the pursuit of God-given goals are distorted into an unhealthy preoccupation with our own welfare. The healthy belief in our value as children of God and recipients of his grace is distorted into an unhealthy sense of our own rights.

In other words, we think we deserve special treatment. Regularly.

Every manifestation of anger requires us to look deeply inside at our underlying attitudes. But when it comes to circumstantial anger that is often driven by egoism, preoccupation with our own welfare or an extreme sense of our rights, a careful examination of our attitudes is essential. Our character growth depends on it.

Few if any of us escape an occasional (perhaps more than occasional!) descent into this form of anger. I wish I could say that after thirty years as a Christian and more than twenty-five years in church leadership, I have got to the point where I always respond to frustrating circumstances maturely. But I don't. Because I believe that this form of anger is so prevalent, I want to tell a rather embarrassing story that reveals the truth about some of my immature attitudes and highlights the way in which God's truth and wisdom can guide us through this kind of anger.

Losing perspective

It all started when I was flying back from a lengthy speaking tour in Europe. Just as the plane reached the gate at O'Hare airport in Chicago, I heard the following announcement over the P.A. system of the 747: 'Bill Hybels, please go to the airline representative in the arrival lounge as soon as you leave the plane.'

What would you think if you were summoned in that rather urgent manner on a 747 after a long international flight? Wouldn't you assume it was something serious? I knew that while I was en route from Europe, Todd and Shauna had been flying home for Thanksgiving on separate planes from the West Coast. I knew that Lynne was driving home late at night from Michigan, where she had been visiting her parents. I immediately assumed that some kind of tragedy had befallen my wife or children while travelling. I was beginning to picture a family gathering very different from the one I had been anticipating.

Then I thought, *Maybe it isn't a family crisis. Maybe a tragedy has struck our church.* I had been looking forward to our holiday services as a joyful time for our entire congregation. Now what might they be like? What might have gone wrong?

I hurried off the plane and introduced myself to the waiting airline representative. He said, 'Oh, yes, Mr Hybels, I'm sorry to tell you that we've lost one of your suitcases. You checked two cases onto this flight and only one of them made it. We are very sorry. We know you travel a lot, and we hate to have this happen to our regular passengers. We just wanted to let you know that you will have to go to the lost luggage counter and give them a description of your suitcase.'

After his first sentence, I didn't care what else the man said. All I could think was, *It's just a lost suitcase. Thank you, God.* I can't tell you how relieved I was. It could easily have been the greatest tragedy of my life, and it turned out to be a silly lost case. I was so grateful.

With that trauma behind me, I followed the crowd of people through immigration and customs and made my way to the conveyor belt to await my one case that supposedly was put on the plane. While I stood there, I had a little time to think through my recent trauma. What would it have been like to hear the words I thought I was going to hear? What would I have done? I have always imagined that nothing could be worse than hearing that one of my family members had been hurt or killed. How thankful I was not to have heard those words. I tend to get rather impatient waiting for my baggage, but that night I didn't mind having a little time to reflect and recuperate.

As it turned out, however, I ended up having a rather long time to reflect ... and then an even longer time. I began to wonder if either of my suitcases had been put on the plane.

As I began to feel sufficiently recovered from my recent trauma, I began to sense that old feeling of impatience rising up within me. I continued to think about my lost suitcase. *If one of my cases made it on this flight (assuming it did!), why didn't the other one make it? Is it too much to ask the luggage handler to put case B on the conveyor belt alongside case A? Is that so difficult? Or did he leave case B sitting on the tarmac because the bell rang for his coffee break? Did he not care that somebody in Chicago was going to end up with a missing case? Did he think his cup of coffee was more important than my case of clothes?*

As I stood there and watched everyone else pick up their suitcases and head for the exit, my mental attack on the luggage handler continued: *I'd really like to find that man. I'd like to give him a Bible study he'd never forget.*

By now I was warming up, and then my thoughts spun off onto another negative tangent. *Wait a minute. That was a fully-loaded 747. Do you mean to tell me there were three hundred people on that plane and I was the only person whose suitcase wasn't put on it? What did I do wrong? Why is this happening to me? I was in Europe helping churches, for heaven's sake. I was on a mission for God! And this is what I get?*

Oh dear. Distorted thinking. Egoism. Rights. I had to admit how far I was going with those attitudes. But as I watched the few remaining people load up their trolleys and leave, my suitcase still hadn't come. The longer I stood there the more upset I became. An older lady in front of me was pulling numerous cases off the conveyor belt and struggling to get them onto her trolley. The thought crossed my mind, *Do it yourself, woman. At least you've got all your cases. What are you complaining about?* I did eventually help her, but not very joyfully.

Then a European man next to me lit a cigarette, apparently unaware that he was in a non-smoking airport. I didn't have the courage to say anything to him (he was about twice my size), but I gave him my most self-righteous and condescending stare. What I wanted to say to him was, 'You nicotine junkie, don't you know that we don't smoke in public places over here? Do what you want to on your side of the Atlantic, but this is America! I hope you get arrested. One night in Cook County Jail will sort you out!'

Remember I said earlier that the first step in managing anger is to become aware of it? At about this point in my story, I realized that I had crossed the line from being mildly annoyed to being down-right angry. I could not deny that my fuse had been lit. All the tell-tale signs were there. I could feel my internal temperature rising. My collar was getting warm. My pulse rate was increasing and my breathing pattern changing. *If I'm not careful*, I thought, *I might actually lose my temper!*

I am not saying I should have felt that way. I am only saying that I did. And at that point the most important thing for me to do was to recognize that, to admit that what was going on inside me was anger. Acknowledging that gave me the opportunity to slow down and say, *Wait a minute. Why am I so angry about a lost suitcase and a few delays? What is going on here?*

Finally my case arrived. Then I had the pleasure of looking for the lost-luggage counter so I could fill out numerous forms, which is not my favourite activity, especially when my body is operating on London time, which was about 1.00 a.m.

As I walked in the general direction of the lost-luggage department and began to reflect on the anger I had so astutely identified, I realized that I had an important decision to make, and I had just a few minutes in which to make it. What was I going to do with my anger when I came face to face with the person at the lost-luggage counter. That, I knew, would be my moment of truth. As I walked, I was running through my options, determining just how much of a fool I was going to be.

The voice of wisdom

As I said earlier, we always have choices about how to handle our anger. I knew that as I walked down that long hallway. I knew I could choose to deny my anger and repress it. I could pretend I was a super-Christian who never got angry. I could put a smile on my face and cover up what was going on underneath. But I figured that probably my true feelings would seep out all over the place and poison the conversation anyway, so repression wasn't a good option.

Or I could choose to nurse my anger until I was worked up enough to start spewing it out. I could take the path of least resistance and do what felt good at the moment. I could satisfy my dark desire to make somebody else pay for my inconvenience. But I knew I would regret that later.

The third option was to slow down and continue reflecting. I could try to discern the underlying attitudes that were driving my anger. I could think about Scripture verses that addressed and perhaps overturned my underlying attitudes. I could pray and ask God to give me assistance with the crisis at hand. I could bring to mind mature Christians who are good models of effective anger management and imagine how they would handle the problem.

Make no mistake. I did have options, options that would either dishonour God and hurt other people or honour God and build my character. The question was, Which option would I choose?

As I walked past what seemed like a mile of conveyor belts, I was contemplating that very question. As I approached the lost-luggage counter I could see a young woman standing behind the counter. With each step towards her my internal battle continued. Two parallel thoughts raced through my mind. One said, *I want to vent my frustration all over that woman. I want her to know how maddening it is to have a lost bag late at night after a transatlantic flight. I know I will feel better if I can make somebody pay.*

But another part of me was listening to the quiet whisper of God that was steadily chipping away at my distorted attitudes and twisted perspectives. 'Bill,' God seemed to say, 'twenty minutes ago when that message came over the P.A. you thought maybe your wife or one of the children had been killed. You thought a terrible tragedy had struck your church. And when you found out it was just a lost suitcase, you were so grateful. You whispered a prayer to me, saying, "Thank you, Father. It's just a lost case." Bill, you have got to put this back in perspective. It *is* just a lost case. And remember, the airline was kind enough to warn you that they had lost your suitcase. They apologized in the arrival lounge. They were trying to help you through all this.'

God continued, 'Bill, this is not that woman's fault. She didn't lose your case. As a matter of fact, she stands behind that counter for long hours and low wages and takes abuse from annoyed passengers who have never learned to manage their anger. She doesn't need any more from you.'

I sensed a final thought from God as I approached the woman. 'You have never looked in the eyes of someone who does not matter to me. You have never made eye contact with someone for whom my Son did not give his life. Your personal creed for twenty-five years has been that people matter to me – *all* people, no matter who they are. So they ought to be treated as though they matter. Regardless of your personal frustrations, you ought to treat people as the treasures they are to me.'

That was very hard to hear. How could I get so caught up in my petty frustrations that I forgot that the battle going on in my mind was not only about me? In this case, as in most cases, our expressions of anger involve another person, and that person matters to God. Obviously the woman behind the lost-luggage counter didn't have anything to do with the event that caused my anger, but even if she had, even if she had been wholly responsible for losing my suitcase, she would still be one of God's children who deserves to be treated with respect, dignity, grace and love. How could I have forgotten this?

In that moment God was whispering to me what I believe he whispers to each of us in those critical moments of decision: 'Come on, handle this one the right way. Remember that you're dealing with one of my beloved children. Do the right thing.'

So I arrived at the counter. With God's words lingering in my mind, I made the decision not to lash out at this woman. I walked up and put my bag down quietly. The woman must have sensed some stress in my appearance because without my saying anything, she said, softly and kindly, 'Have you had a bad day?'

I thought, *This woman puts me to shame. She has probably had loads of abuse already today, and up walks another obviously stressed-out person with a complaint. And yet she greets me like this. What style!*

The writer of Proverbs says that 'a kind-hearted woman gains respect,' and it's true (11:16). The writer also says that 'a gentle answer turns away wrath, but a harsh word stirs up anger' (15:1). That is true too. That woman had no way of knowing the battle that had been raging in my mind during the previous twenty minutes, but she greeted me with a gentle tone and a kind word.

I don't know what I would have done if she had said, 'And what's the matter with you?' I hope I would have focused even more intently on God's words and proceeded in a God-honouring way. But I don't know that I would. All I know is that her kind spirit helped me to continue on the right path. We need to remember this when we are experiencing conflict with our spouse or children or colleagues. We have the power, with our gentle tones and kind words, to lower the temperature in any angry person.

I could feel that happening to me, as I replied, 'Yes, a bad day.' But I couldn't even say *that* truthfully; her kindness, along with God's promptings, was continuing to chip away at my distorted attitudes. After a moment I said, 'Actually, it was a good day with just a bad ending with this lost suitcase.'

She said, 'Well, you have some work to do now. You have to fill out a few forms.'

'I know,' I said. 'I've been through this before.' So I took the forms and began describing the colour and size of the case and giving all the other necessary

245

information. When I finished, I passed the forms back to her.

She looked me in the eye and, with a hint of a smile, said, 'Shall I have this suitcase delivered to your home, or shall we send it to Willow Creek Community Church?' She smiled again and said, 'I go there.'

Whew! I thought. *Thank God I did this one right*! Had I handled myself differently ... well, you get the picture. We chatted for a few moments. As I left she smiled again and said, 'Happy Thanksgiving, Bill.'

Getting it right

Later that night I thanked God for the whole ordeal, because it taught me so much about myself. I learnt that within twenty minutes I can go from earnestly thanking God that I was not facing a horrible tragedy to being really angry and ready to damage an innocent person all because of a lost suitcase.

I am so sinful. Under the right conditions, I am still capable of going from light to darkness. After almost three decades of being a Christian, my heart still needs so much work. I amaze myself!

But that experience taught me something on the positive side too. I learnt what a difference it makes when I listen to God and let him address my distorted attitudes and my twisted perspectives. Without the work of the Holy Spirit in my life, I will sin in my anger. That is a fact I cannot deny. But when I yield to his work and follow him through the steps of constructive anger management, I can control my spirit; I can get it right.

And I love the feeling of getting it right! I love being able to look back on a frustrating situation without having to regret my behaviour. I know well what that kind of regret feels like. It's a terrible feeling. Every time I have mismanaged my anger, I have ended up saying, 'I don't want to be that kind of man. I don't want to do that kind of damage. I don't want to dishonour God in that way.' My guess is that you feel the same way every time you sin in your anger.

The good news is that we can break out of old habits of sin. Every time we find ourselves responding to the circumstances of life with anger, we have an opportunity to grow spiritually, develop character and honour God. It won't be easy; it is definitely one of life's postgraduate-level courses. But with God's help, we can 'be angry and not sin'.

12
Trust God in everything

The book of Proverbs can be summarized in one brief passage that has probably been memorized by more of Christ's followers than almost any other passage in the Bible. If you have any church background, you can probably quote these two short verses faster than I can write them out. They are Proverbs 3:5–6: 'Trust in the LORD with all your heart and lean not on your own understanding; in all your ways acknowledge him, and he will make your paths straight.' I consider this the crowning proverb of all the proverbs not just because it is familiar to so many people but because it has had such far-reaching impact in my own life.

Soon after I became a Christian, I did what most new believers do: I quietly considered how seriously I intended to take my new-found faith. I realized that Jesus had died for me, and I wanted to show my gratitude to God by trying to walk with him. But to what extent? I knew I should read my Bible a little bit. I knew I should pray now and then. I knew I should get somewhat involved in my church. But how far did I need to take all this?

I knew a few people who were becoming flat-out, totally devoted, full-blown Christians. Almost overnight, it seemed, their faith was altering everything: their morals, their relationships, their money management – in some cases, even their careers. This seemed a little extreme to me. I was quite sure I didn't want to go that far. But how far did I want to go? To what extent did I want my new faith to affect my everyday life?

About that time a mature Christian man who knew me well sensed my struggle. 'Bill,' he said, 'I have a challenge for you. Why not put your whole life in God's hands? Why not trust him fully? Why not stake your life on him? Why not let him lead and guide you in every area of your life for as long as he proves himself trustworthy? If at any point he shows himself to be untrustworthy, then you can bail out, turn your back – whatever. But until that time, give God the opportunity to lead and guide your life. Give him a chance to prove himself trustworthy.'

This man knew me well enough to know I was never one to back down from a stiff challenge. I think he also knew what I knew deep inside: that I would never be content unless I took the risk of trusting God fully. If God was who he said he was, he obviously knew a lot more about me and my future than I knew. What a fool I would be to pass up the chance to access his knowledge and insight and guidance.

What might God have in mind for my life? Where might he want me to go? What might he want me to do or to become? What if he had extraordinary plans for a seventeen-year-old boy from Kalamazoo, Michigan? What if he had fascinating people he wanted me to meet? What if he had a risky career in mind for me? What if he had challenges and adventures I couldn't even imagine waiting for me? What if I missed all this because I wasn't willing to give his wisdom and his guidance a try?

It doesn't exactly sound like prayerful consideration, does it? It wasn't. It was more like taking a dare or making a wise bet. I took a purely pragmatic view and worked out that there were minimal negative risks. The man had said I could get out any time the system didn't seem to be working, any time God proved himself untrustworthy. I half expected that to happen, but I looked at the positive possibilities, and I decided there was little to lose. I might as well go for it. So I said, 'All right, God, I am making a decision today. I am going to give your leadership a try. I am all yours.'

I know how arrogant this sounds, a seventeen-year-old boy deciding to 'give God's leadership a try', as if I were doing him a favour. But that was roughly how I saw it as a young Christian. How grateful I am that God peered beneath the exterior of my life into a heart and soul that desperately needed him. How grateful I am that he was willing to respond to my calculated approach to faith with the gifts of his love and his guidance.

Why am I so grateful? Because the day I made that deal with God, and he with me, was the beginning of the greatest adventure of my life. I shudder to think of what I would have missed had I made a different choice.

The same opportunity is open to all of us. Anyone can make the same decision to trust God, to 'give God's leadership a try'. He accepts all of us where we are, with all our doubts and reservations firmly in place – just the way he accepted me. We have to trust him just one day at a time. As my friend put it, we have to trust him only as long as he proves himself trustworthy.

Trust in the Lord

Maybe you're almost ready to make this decision, but you have a few questions. Maybe you look at the first part of Proverbs 3:5–6 ('Trust in the Lord with all your heart'), and you think you would like to try that, but you are not quite sure what it means. How would you begin trusting God on a daily basis?

Perhaps it will help to imagine a relationship you had in the past. Think back to a young man or woman who made your heart miss a beat. Can you remember the day you first summoned the courage to ask that person out? Or to accept such an invitation?

During those first interactions you were undoubtedly watching closely to see how trustworthy the new focus of your romantic interest was. Whether you were consciously testing that person or doing so on a subconscious level, you were fitting together the various components of what you saw in that person in order to determine whether or not this was someone you could really trust.

If he said he would be at your house at 7.00 p.m., you were quite relieved when he turned up on time. Had he turned up an hour late without so much as a mention of his tardiness, you probably would have cringed, even if only on the inside. Punctuality may seem like a small thing, but deep inside you knew it was an indication of a person's trustworthiness. How could you entrust the deeper issues of your life to someone who wasn't even trustworthy enough to turn up on time?

But let's assume your friend turned up on time and proved trustworthy in regard to other relatively minor issues in life. The next step in developing trust was probably to take some risks in conversation and discuss a few matters of the heart. As the other person spoke, you listened carefully, trying to discern the ring of truth in his or her words. Did this person's thoughts, ideas and descriptions of experiences seem well-grounded and believable, or did they sound far-fetched and rather detached from reality?

And when you spoke honestly and openly, did that person listen carefully and respond appropriately? Did he or she offer good insights, heartfelt compassion, thoughtful affirmations or necessary challenges? The nature of that conversation and every conversation that followed either increased or eroded your trust in this person.

If your trust grew to the point where you decided to go out with this person exclusively, then the trust test continued on a higher level. It had to. The greater the commitment involved in a relationship, the greater the level of trust that is required. What began as attention to your partner's punctuality and later as attention to the trustworthiness of what he or she said has grown into a concern over issues like long-term loyalty, truthfulness and dependability. As the commitments become broader and the confidences deeper, the breadth and depth of trust must similarly increase. That is part of what it means to make life work in relationships. And we can't sit passively waiting for trust to grow. Building trust requires action. We need to take little steps and then assess the progress. We need to take little risks and then evaluate the consequences.

After engaging in that process for months, perhaps even years, we come to a point where we can say, 'I can fully trust this person. I have no doubt about that. I have had the opportunity to confirm this person's trustworthiness time and time again in experience after experience. As far as I am concerned, the proof of the pudding is in the eating. This person is a trustworthy friend!' Or time and experience may force us to conclude that a certain person cannot be trusted. We have seen too many inconsistencies of character in that person and have witnessed too much irresponsible behaviour. In relationship with him or her we have experienced too many disappointments. All the indications tell us that this person is a bad risk.

To trust or not to trust. This is no small decision, nor is it a decision we make all at once. I think of it less as a decision than as a gradual move towards a given conclusion, a conclusion based on hundreds of personal interactions and countless hours of deep reflection.

253

The big step

It is similar in our relationship with God. 'Trust in the LORD with all your heart,' says the writer of this proverb. But that is no simple pronouncement. There is no short cut to trust. Though we can and should find cause for trust as we read the biblical record of God's trustworthy behaviour throughout history, there is a more personal dimension of trust in God that we must develop in the same way that we develop trust with friends, boy and girlfriends or spouses: by sharing our everyday lives with him deeply and genuinely over a long period of time. That is the only way to determine for ourselves if it is safe and wise to entrust our lives to God.

Even as you have been turning the pages of this book, you have probably been gauging your trust. As you have read and reflected on the biblical passages I have quoted, on the stories I have told about other people's lives and on my experiences, you have undoubtedly found yourself being either more or less willing to trust God. I hope that you have been falling on the *more* side rather than the *less* side. If you are not yet a Christian, I hope that you are coming closer and closer to believing that the Bible is true, that God is who he says he is and that Jesus is the Saviour of the world.

Some of you may have been hearing a quiet whisper as you have read. You may not be ready to believe this, but the Spirit of God has a reputation for speaking words of truth into the stillness of our spirits. 'I am real,' he may be saying to you. 'This whole thing is true. I love you. If you will take a tiny step of trust, I will prove myself trustworthy. How about it?'

Where are you in your spiritual journey? Has God proved himself to you to the extent that you are ready for the next step of faith? If this is new to you, the next step may be a big one, but the truth is that you cannot make progress in your relationship with God until you take it. John 1:12 says that 'to all who received him, to those who believed in his name, he gave the right to become children of God'. Sooner or later, every person who is investigating Christianity and finding God trustworthy has to take that big step of personally receiving the message of Christ and believing that he is who he claims to be, the Son of God whose life and death open the way for us to be adopted into the family of God.

Romans 10:13 tells us that 'everyone who calls on the name of the Lord will be saved'. The word *everyone* reveals that God intends to be inclusive. But those two key words 'who calls' remind us that we have to take action in response to God's gracious intention. He offers us forgiveness, but we need to acknowledge that we need it and then willingly accept it. He offers wise and loving leadership for our lives, but we have to let him know that we want it. He offers the gift, but we need to extend our hands and take hold of it.

Many people come to the point of decision and ask, 'What if I call upon God to forgive my sins and to lead my life, and I discover there is no one at home in heaven? What if nothing happens? What if there is only silence?' My only response is that there is just one way to find out: Take the step and see if God proves himself trustworthy. If there is only silence from heaven, you have your answer. You gave it a try and it didn't work. Apparently it wasn't real. Now you are free to walk away, and you never have to look back.

This could happen. You could sincerely seek God and find that he is not there. Though the promises of Scripture and the experiences of millions of people throughout history strongly suggest otherwise and give us ample reason for believing that God is there, they do not offer us ultimate proof. Taking the big step towards God always involves an act of faith. But look at it this way: a life worth living requires many steps of faith.

On my first skydiving experience, I turned to my instructor, patted my parachute and said, 'Can I really trust this thing to open?' He said, 'There's only one way to find out.' Then he chuckled and added, 'All I can say is that mine has never failed me yet.' Moments later we were both hurtling toward earth at an extremely high speed. Obviously my parachute opened, and so did his.

Though the stakes in skydiving are high – life and death hang upon a ripcord – and the thrill is tremendous, it is an optional experience. If it seems too frightening to us, we don't have to do it. Unless the challenge and the pleasure entice us, there is no good reason to exercise our faith by jumping out of an aeroplane at five thousand feet.

But deciding how to respond to Christ's offer of salvation is not optional. Eternity hangs in the balance, and we have to choose. Either choice requires faith. Choosing to place our trust in Christ demands faith in a Creator and Sustainer and Lover and Saviour we cannot see or hear or feel with our senses. Turning away from Christ's offer demands either faith in our own sufficiency to face the God of eternity alone or faith in a godless universe. Which way do you want to go with your faith?

I could tell you story after story of people who have chosen to place their faith in God and have experienced a conversion reaching to the depths of their soul. For some people this is an emotional experience; for others it is not. A businessman who had recently accepted Christ's forgiveness told me, 'It feels like a lawsuit has just been dropped – the heavy sense of judgment that had hung over my head for years is gone.' Other people testify to a deep sense of peace or a serenity of soul unlike anything they have ever known.

I experienced such a conversion at a Christian camp when I was seventeen. I am not a particularly feeling-oriented person, and I certainly wasn't as a teenager. But when I called out for the Saviour of the world to be my personal Saviour, something happened in the following thirty seconds that was totally unexpected. I didn't get emotional. I didn't cry or scream or laugh, as some people do in a sincere, outward expression of internal change. But I did experience such a pure, rich, deep filling of divine love that I thought I was going to explode. I felt like I had to tell somebody about this, so I woke up some of my friends, dragged them out of bed and told them what happened. 'I just invited Christ into my life, and I feel so different inside. I can't find words to explain what happened, but I know it was real.'

In Luke 15:10 Jesus says, 'I tell you, there is rejoicing in the presence of the angels of God over one sinner who repents.' I wasn't aware of the angels' celebration that night, but I couldn't miss my friends' excitement. I hadn't realized that many of them had been praying for a long time that I would take this very step. Needless to say, they were effusive in their encouragement, and our celebrating went on long into the night.

What about you? Are you ready to take the big step of faith? You can do it by praying a simple prayer: 'Jesus Christ, I need a Saviour. I need someone to forgive my sins and to lead me in my life. Please do that for me.'

Some of you may have done that long ago, but then you turned away from God's leadership; for whatever reason, you went back to trying to live life on your own. But now you are ready to ask for God's forgiveness and to trust once again in his leadership. If you're ready to do that, please don't hold back. Tell God that you need his help and his guidance and that you are rededicating yourself to him. He is waiting to hear those words.

Mental files

I am confident that anyone who acts on faith will find God to be trustworthy for salvation. But that is only the beginning. The next step is to trust God in the many decisions of everyday life. Throughout this book, I have compared two paths, one based on human wisdom, the other based on God's. I have done my best to build a compelling case for the superiority of God's wisdom.

I have tried to convince you that taking initiative is better than being passive or lazy or fatalistic; that doing good beats the soul-numbing alternative of self-absorption; that self-discipline, though difficult to develop, pays rich dividends; that speaking the truth in love is better than spinning webs of deceit; that choosing friends wisely is a significant key to growing in wisdom; that marrying well is the foundation of a marriage that lasts; that forging strong families is the best way to pass a positive legacy from one generation to the next; that cultivating compassion is a powerful way to change the world; and that managing anger constructively is vital to personal happiness and harmony in relationships.

The book of Proverbs has taught me so much about how to live my life, and I hope I have been effective in passing on what I have learned. But the question remains, Will we choose God's path in the various decisions of daily life? Will we trust God enough to conform our wills to his ways?

It has been almost thirty years since I made the decision to try to entrust my entire life to God, and I am more convinced today of God's trustworthiness than I have ever been in my life. As I look back over the years, I have no regrets about the times I followed God's path. Not a single one. Sometimes it was hard; sometimes it was confusing. But always, in the end, I was glad I had chosen God's wisdom.

On the other hand, I could fill volumes with the regret I carry for the times I wilfully chose another path. A file in my mind called 'My Very Stupid File' is filled with the memories of all the times I came to critical crossroads in my life and chose a foolish path.

Each time, I would end up saying, 'That was so stupid. Look at the consequences. Look at the people I have hurt. Look at the guilt I carry. Look at the time I have lost. Refusing to go God's way was *so stupid.*'

As I said in the first chapter of this book, we are not born wise; we are born with folly in our hearts and minds. One of the main tasks of life is to grow out of folly and into wisdom. Part of that growth process involves learning from mistakes. So whenever I learned a lesson from my foolish choices that allowed me to make a wise choice the next time I came to a similar crossroads, I mentally put those choices into 'My Very Clever File'. Frequently perusing and comparing my two files was one of my most effective ways of building trust in God. It was obvious that every time I went God's way, my life worked better. Every time I trusted him by obeying his commands, working according to his wisdom or yielding to his guidance, he proved to be worthy of my trust: his wisdom worked, and his commands were just, and his guidance served me well. Eventually I was able to say without hesitation, 'I do trust the Lord with all my heart! I am not fooling myself or making false claims. I trust God because he has proved himself to be trustworthy.'

Lean not on your own understanding

What does the second section of Proverbs 3:5–6 mean? When the Bible tells us to 'lean not on our own understanding', does that mean we have to throw our brains away in order to grow as Christians? Does it mean we have to discount our discernment and assume that we have no understanding of anything, that we have learnt nothing during the course of our lives? Of course not. But it does caution us to be wary of our reflex human reactions to the complex issues of life. Whether we want to acknowledge it or not, human perspective is always limited, and natural intuition is always slightly suspect. If the truth be told, we will all mess up our lives to some degree if we merely follow our own insights. We need God's input in the decision-making of everyday life.

I recently read an article called '178 Seconds to Live'. It was about twenty pilots who were capable pilots in clear weather but who had never taken instrument training. Each was put in a flight simulator and instructed to do whatever he could to keep the aeroplane under control as he flew into thick, dark clouds and stormy weather. The article stated that all twenty pilots 'crashed' and 'killed themselves' within an average of 178 seconds. It took these seasoned pilots with skilled intuition less than three minutes to destroy themselves once they lost their visual reference points!

Not long ago, I was helping to fly a plane on a night trip back to Chicago from the East Coast. While the pilot in command was busy entering data into the computer, I did the take-off and climb, and then kept us straight and level and on course. All was going well until we entered a very thick layer of clouds. Having no reference point outside the plane, I calmly focused on the instruments on the panel and made whatever corrections they called for. But several minutes after entering 'the soup', the instruments called for me to make a correction that seemed all wrong to me; they indicated that we were slowly banking to the left. I knew, however, that I had not altered the controls even slightly, and I was confident that there had been no wind changes or turbulence of any kind. So I sat there and said to myself, 'There is no way we can be banking to the left.' And I did not make the corrections called for by the instruments.

My rationale was simple: I had been flying since I was fifteen years old – ordinary planes, seaplanes, single-engine planes, multi-engine planes, turbo-props, jets, even helicopters – without a single mishap or close call. I assumed that since I had done so much flying and had maintained such a good record I had obviously developed a dependable sense of intuition about an aeroplane's motion. So, on that particular night, I made the deliberate choice to trust my own intuition over the indications coming from the instruments on the panel. I said, 'I know better. If it comes down to a choice between the instruments and my own intuition, I'll trust my intuition.'

It was a bad choice. Fortunately, about that time, the pilot looked up from his charts, looked at the instruments, grabbed the controls and made an immediate correction. He gave me a sidelong glance that seemed to be asking, 'Are you crazy?' Then he gave me a wry smile, pointed to the instruments, and said, 'Believe those things. We'll both live longer.' For the rest of the flight, I kept my eyes glued to the instruments, and you can be sure that I made every slight correction they called for.

When the writer of this proverb tells us not to lean

on our own understanding, he is making the point that no matter how clever we are or how many life experiences we have under our belts, we still need to realize that human judgment is always limited and sometimes wrong. Sometimes our best notions about what ought to be said or done are ill-advised, dangerous, even destructive. When it comes to the key decisions in our lives, we almost always need deeper insights and a broader perspective than mere human wisdom can offer us.

What we desperately need is God's mind on the serious matters of life. He offers it to us through the teaching of his Word and the inner guidance of his Spirit. Our job is not to question it or to assume that we know better, like an over-confident pilot who overrules the instructions of his instruments, but to trust that God does know better how to make our lives work. A helpful spiritual rule of thumb might be, 'When in doubt, always, always, always trust the wisdom of God.'

In all your ways acknowledge him

Let's get right to the point of this next phrase. In the context of this passage, 'to acknowledge God' means to acknowledge his wisdom, his insight and his understanding. That is what this book has been about. 'In all our ways' means ... well, in *all* our ways. We can be assured that any area of life we decide to manage without the benefit of God's wisdom, insight and understanding is going to end up creating a problem. Any area in which we put up a *No Trespassing* sign and try to keep God out will probably be the area that imperils the quality of our lives and threatens those around us. It doesn't take many holes to sink a ship. Just one. And it doesn't even have to be a big one.

Some people look at their career ambitions, others at their sexuality, still others at their money, or their choice of friends or their leisure-time activities, and they say, 'I know all about your wisdom, God. I know what the Bible says about this. I know how your Spirit is prompting me. But the answer is no. I don't want your advice. I don't want your wisdom. I'll manage this area on my own.'

Remember the chapter on initiative? Remember the people who patted themselves on the back for taking initiative in almost every area of life, maybe even nine out of ten, but failed to realize the damage that a single area of laziness could do? This principle bears repeating. Nine out of ten is not enough, whether it refers to taking initiative or to any other form of character building or obedience. Just one area of life in which we refuse God's wisdom can have far-reaching negative consequences. In time it will almost surely have an adverse effect on other dimensions of our lives as well. Eventually, when life is no longer working well, we will probably look back and say, 'It all started with this one little private area that I thought I could manage better than God . . . and now this.'

Many people seem determined to learn everything the hard way. But we could all save ourselves and others enormous trouble if we could learn what millions of people have learned before us: Any area of life that is not placed under God's leadership and wisdom will eventually be the source of great frustration, heartache and pain.

The writer of Proverbs pleads with us not to subject ourselves to this kind of risk. If we acknowledge God in all our ways, in every area of our lives, we can significantly lower the risk of trouble. It is like patching up the one hole that is threatening to sink our ship.

Do you have any private areas that you have not yet yielded to God? If so, why not turn them over to God? Take down the *No Trespassing* sign and let God in. I have never met a person who has regretted this decision. It is your move. I cheer you on.

And he will make your paths straight

Before this last line of the passage sends anyone off on a tangent, I want to be clear about what it does not mean. It does not mean that God will necessarily make us healthy, wealthy and happy. It does not mean that he will make us comfortable, popular and slim. It does not mean that he will satisfy all our trivial wishes and desires. 'He will make your paths straight' means that he will give our lives direction, purpose, focus and fulfilment. He will guide us around swamps and ditches so we can stay on the right path. He will work in us to transform our hearts and souls. He will work through us to have an impact on others. And when we die, he will lead us straight through the gates of heaven. When you think about it, what more could we ask for?

I recently attended the funeral of the father of one of my closest friends. It was held in the sanctuary of the church I attended throughout my childhood and teenage years. Everything looked exactly the way it had thirty years earlier. As I sat there my mind was flooded with memories.

I thought particularly of the older man who had challenged me to trust God with all my heart and to allow him to guide and direct my life. As I thought back on what that had meant during the previous thirty years of my life, I could barely contain my emotions. I smiled as I realized that I could not recall spending a single night in the past three decades tossing and turning over a lack of fulfilment or meaning or purpose or adventure.

Then I choked back the tears as I thought of all I would probably have missed had I chosen to manage life on my own: work that makes me excited to get up in the morning, friends who have become like family to me, a constantly growing marriage and children who provide some of the greatest joys of my life.

In that funeral service, I put my hands on my knees with my palms up, and I said, 'God, my life is probably more than half over, but I want to make the same deal regarding whatever time I have left that I made regarding the past. I want to trust you with all my heart and lean not on my own understanding. In all my ways, I want to acknowledge you, and I want to trust you to make my paths straight.' I can't describe the sense of peace and hope that flooded my soul. If the future is anything like the last thirty years, it is going to be wonderful!

Don't miss the adventure

I love Jeremiah 29:11, in which God says, 'I know the plans I have for you. . . . They are plans for good and not for evil, to give you a future and a hope' (LB). I love to reflect on this verse. I love to think about God designing a plan specifically for my life. I love to let this truth sink deeply into my soul.

God has a plan, a future and a hope, for each of us, with our own name on it. Though God doesn't promise a life free from problems or pain, he does promise a life that is too good to miss. But we will never discover that life – that adventure – until we entrust ourselves to his guidance and leadership. God knows us better than we know ourselves. He understands our capabilities and our limitations. He knows exactly what pitfalls we need to avoid and sees the full extent of our potential. He sets his sights high for us, and he is willing to give us every form of assistance we need to live out his perfectly designed plan. But we need to turn to him and trust him fully.

Whatever step of faith you need to take, I hope and pray that you will take it. I don't know what God has in store for your life, but I do know that it is an adventure you won't want to miss!

Questions for reflection and discussion

Introduction and Chapter 1:
Pursue wisdom

1. How would you define *wisdom*?

2. The author suggests that Proverbs is not a collection of promises or rigid rules about life but rather a group of comments about how life usually works. What difference will this make to how we read Proverbs?

3. How can having a wise parent, a wise child, a wise employer or a wise employee make a difference to someone?

4. The opposite of a wise person, says Proverbs, is a fool. What examples of foolish decisions or behaviour have you observed in the news lately?

5. One element of wisdom is understanding that actions have consequences. Why does it some-

times seem so hard for people to live by that principle?

6. The book of Proverbs begins with the famous summary statement, 'The fear of the Lord is the beginning of wisdom' (1:7). What is meant by that?

7. Consider how Proverbs guided the author through a difficult relationship and through the wise use of his money early in his marriage. What strikes you most from these examples and why?

8. What do you hope to learn from the book of Proverbs?

Chapter 2: Take initiative

1. Jesus' parable about the financial agent in Luke 16 is rather startling. Do you think his point is to commend the taking of initiative? Explain.

2. Why do people often fail to take initiative to solve their problems? Why do they get stuck in ruts?

3. The author says one symptom of 'sluggardliness' is to put things off till later. In what ways or areas do you tend to procrastinate and why?

4. Why do we sometimes engage in 'selective sluggardliness'?

5. If we do identify an area that needs some diligence and initiative, this can sometimes mean we'll have to eliminate something else in order to

give time and attention to our area of 'selective sluggardliness.' How can we got about deciding what we should eliminate so we can give our efforts to something else that is more important?

6. One area the author suggests we consider is that of relationships that are troubled or tense. What have you found that helps you to take steps in making peace under such circumstances?

7. Regarding work, Colossians 3:23 is quoted: 'Whatever you do, work at it with all your heart, as working for the Lord, not for men.' What do you think it means to work for the Lord?

8. The third area considered is that of our physical well-being. What does it mean to honour God with our bodies?

9. The author suggests that we can be careless with money whether we've got a little or a lot. Do you agree or disagree? Explain.

10. Finally, what does it mean to be rich towards God?

11. How can you increase your wealth towards God?

12. What step or steps do you think God has been leading you to take as a result of having considered the ideas in this chapter?

Chapter 3: Do good

1. When have you felt good after helping someone in need? What was the experience like?

2. Proverbs 3:27 says we should not withhold good from those who deserve it. How can we tell if someone deserves help or not?

3. When might helping someone actually do more harm than good?

4. How can you tell in advance if that might be the case?

5. The author says that people who are 'exchanging favours' are not really doing good in the sense Proverbs has in mind. Do you agree or disagree, and if so, why?

6. How does the parable of the good Samaritan indicate that there are boundaries to how far we should help people?

7. How can doing good in a community context also help to keep us from burning out?

8. Why is spiritual refreshment such an important part of giving us the energy we need to do good?

9. How have you found that to be true for you?

10. What do you need to do either to create boundaries for yourself in the ways you do good or to engage in acts of goodness that are in your power to do?

Chapter 4: Develop discipline

1. How have you seen the beneficial effects of discipline in your life – or in the lives of those near you?

2. Do you think discipline is usually needed to achieve high goals? Explain.

3. How can a high goal increase our motivation to be disciplined in order to achieve it?

4. 'No Pain. No Gain,' the saying goes. Do you agree or disagree with this?

5. When has employing delayed gratification helped you achieve a goal (in education, at work, in a relationship, with God)?

6. The third component of discipline mentioned is that of advance decision-making. In what kinds of circumstances do you think this would be helpful?

7. Why is advance decision-making so often helpful to us?

8. Several times in the chapter the author suggests that discipline can be an effective way to build relationships (with God or with others). Yet discipline can seem so cold and calculated. Do you think discipline is an effective way to build a relationship or not? Why or why not?

9. The last component of discipline mentioned is that of mini-celebrations. What mini-celebrations do you have in your life?

10. As you look over these four components of discipline, which one could be most helpful to you and in what area of your life?

11. How would increased discipline in your life have a beneficial effect on the lives of others near you?

Chapter 5: Speak truth

1. Why do we feel so irritated or hurt when friends or colleagues or politicians don't tell the truth?

2. How does a failure to speak the truth undermine the very foundation of a relationship?

3. The author suggests that 'harmless' half-truths, exaggerations or white lies are really not harmless at all and may be just as problematic as big lies. Do you agree or disagree? Why or why not?

4. Proverbs' first suggestion for lying less is talking less (10:19). Is this a worthwhile and realistic solution? Please explain.

5. How would you go about trying to talk less? In what kinds of situations would you try not to talk as much or what kinds of topics would you stay away from?

6. The other side of telling the truth is being willing to speak a hard but important truth. Why are we sometimes so unwilling to do this?

7. Have you ever tried to talk to someone about an issue that was difficult but significant? What were the results?

8. What did you learn from what went wrong in this conversation?

9. When have you seen someone combine truth and love effectively?

10. Do you think you are the kind of person who

needs to work more on adding love and grace to your words, or are you the type who needs to put more emphasis on truth-telling rather than peacekeeping?

11. What steps can you take to grow in this area?

Chapter 6: Choose friends wisely

1. Describe one of the best friendships you've ever had.

2. How did your friend affect you and change you?

3. The author suggests that there are certain kinds of people we should not make part of our 'personal development team'. Do you agree or disagree with this strategy? Why or why not?

4. Seven characteristics are identified in Proverbs 6:16–19 that mark out people we should not allow into our circle of close friends – people who are arrogant, who lie, who take advantage of the weak, who devise unethical plans, who slander, and who create conflict. How can such people have a negative effect on us?

5. In theory most of us would probably say that we want to avoid such people, but often we are drawn to and are attracted to them anyway. Why do you think that is so?

6. Do you think these seven traits are easy to identify in others or are they sometimes exhibited in more subtle ways? Explain.

7. The first question asked you to describe one of your best friends. How did that friendship start?

8. Think about the kind of person you want to become, the character traits you'd like to develop. Who do you know who exhibits those traits?

9. What steps could you take to get to know that person or persons better?

Chapter 7: Marry well

1. Think of some couples who have been happily married for a number of years. What are some of the elements you see that have made their marriage strong?

2. What are some of the advantages the author mentions in going slowly before deciding to marry?

3. Whether you are married or not, have you ever had people make comments or give subtle hints about their expectations for you regarding marriage? How did this affect you?

4. What do you think are some of the best ways to get to know someone before you marry him or her?

5. If you are married, how did married life turn out to be different from what you expected?

6. Why is spiritual compatibility such an important factor in deciding whom to marry and in married life?

7. Do you think Christians should reject the possibility of marrying someone who is not a Chris-

tian even if all the other factors mentioned in this chapter are positive? Why or why not?

8. The author says that wounds from our background and emotional difficulties can have serious effects on our marriages. Do you agree or disagree? Explain your response.

9. If an engaged or married couple has not worked through such issues from their past, what steps should they take?

10. If you were thinking about getting married, what people could you gather around you to help you work through this decision?

11. If you are married, who can be your Christian community and how can they support you and help you strengthen your life together?

Chapter 8: Forge strong families: Part one

1. What kind of marriage did your parents have?

2. What did you learn from your parents' marriage?

3. How would you like your marriage to be similar and how would you like it to be different?

4. The author suggests that marriage often involves quite a lot of work. Why do you think this might be so?

5. What do you believe are the most helpful ways to improve a marriage and why?

6. Why is a lifelong commitment in marriage so essential to its stability?

7. The author says couples can move beyond stability to joy by building on every foot of common ground between a husband and wife. What good examples of this have you seen in your marriage or other marriages?

8. Why do opposites so often both attract and repel each other?

9. If you are married, in what ways can your spouse help you grow towards wholeness?

10. Why is adultery never a solution to pain in a marriage?

11. What strategies and tactics can be employed to keep oneself from succumbing to sexual temptation?

12. How does a secure marriage promote the security of children?

Chapter 9: Forge strong families: Part two

1. How were you brought up by your parents?

2. What did your parents do well and not so well?

3. It is not uncommon for children to disrespect their parents. How respectful were you of your parents and why?

4. Sometimes parents should be respected because of their position. But the author also suggests that parents should earn the respect of their children. How can this be done?

5. Suggest some ways in which a parent can love a child 'irrationally'.

6. Proverbs 22:15 says that people are born with a predisposition towards rebellion or causing trouble. Do you agree or disagree? Please explain.

7. 'Spare the rod and spoil the child' may be the most famous of the Bible's proverbs (a paraphrase of 13:24). When, if at all, do you think physical discipline is appropriate in parenting?

8. What other types of disciplinary action are effective and why?

9. The author says that children need both love and limits. Why are both needed in effective parenting?

10. How can parents decide when to intervene in a child's decision-making in order to protect him or her from hurtful or destructive decisions, and when should they stand back and let a child learn through the hard lessons of life?

11. Another gift parents can give children is identifying and encouraging their special skills. Who were the people in your life who identified something special in you and how did they encourage your abilities and interests?

12. If you have children, what gifts do you see in them and how can you encourage them? If you do not have children, what gifts do you see in the children in your life (nieces, nephews, neigh-

bours, children of friends), and how can you encourage them?

Chapter 10: Cultivate compassion

1. When have you experienced being the outcast or the one bullied or picked on?

2. Did anyone come to help you? What was that experience like?

3. In many places Proverbs suggests that God has a special concern for the poor. Why do you think this is so?

4. What are some of the ways in which the author says we can open our eyes to the poor?

5. What contact have you had with those who are poor or who are disabled or who live on the edges of society for one reason or another?

6. What other ways could you have your eyes opened to the poor?

7. A second way to develop compassion is actually to get involved in helping needy people. How have you done this and what opportunities are there for you to do it?

8. Sometimes we think of helping existing projects and organizations. What small individual acts (like that of the woman mentioned who paid for someone else's groceries) are possible for you?

9. Money is often the hardest thing for us to give. Why is this so?

10. The author says tithing (giving a tenth of our

income) to a local body of believers is a minimum. Do you agree or disagree? Explain your answer.

11. Building relationships is the last major suggestion offered for cultivating compassion. What relationships have you developed or could you develop?

Chapter 11: Manage anger

1. Ephesians 4:26 says we can be angry without sinning. What do you think this means?

2. When and how can good things come from our being angry?

3. Why is controlling our anger often so difficult?

4. Would you describe yourself as a 'bottler' (someone who holds anger in) or as a 'spewer' (someone who lets anger out)?

5. Why is being a 'bottler' not a solution to anger? What problems arise from bottling up our anger?

6. Why is being a 'spewer' an inadequate solution to anger, that actually leads to other problems?

7. Why is it sometimes hard to acknowledge that we are angry?

8. The author says we should look beneath the surface of the immediate event that triggered our anger to identify the underlying issue or attitude that is at the root of our anger. How can this help us deal constructively with anger?

9. Having identified an underlying issue, what

alternatives are then possible besides bottling up or spewing out our anger?

10. Sometimes our anger (as the story about the lost suitcase illustrates) is due just to inconvenience or unavoidable circumstances. Why do these often bother us so much?

11. What are some good strategies for handling anger in these circumstances?

Chapter 12: Trust God in everything

1. The author considers how you learn to trust someone with whom you are going out. In what ways does this comparison help you understand what it means to trust God?

2. What *does* it mean to trust God?

3. Why is trusting God in this way difficult?

4. Why is it tempting to trust our own judgment instead of God's?

5. What experiences have you had of trusting God?

6. What kinds of items have you put in your 'Very Clever File' or 'Very Stupid File' that you have learned as a result of your experiences with God?

7. What risks are there in trusting God's leadership in life?

8. What benefits can come from making a decision to trust God in this way?

9. The author says that trusting God is like a para-

chute jump in that it always involves an element of faith. Do you agree or not? Explain.

10. Many steps of faith in God are possible, from a first step, to a reaffirmation of an earlier commitment, to a decision to turn over one area of life to God that you had previously labelled 'No Trespassing'. What step of faith might God be asking of you now?